P9-CWD-799

More Praise for *The Elements of Résumé Style*

"Absolutely outstanding. A marvelous piece of work. This book delivers what it says it will and then some. No job seeker or career changer should be without it."

—JOHN J. KENNEDY, ED.D., CAREER DEVELOPMENT CONSULTANT

"Scott has managed the near-impossible—covering the subject from AA to ZZ. For the serious résumé writer, the sections "Request for Salary Requirements" and "Marketing to Yourself" alone are worth fifty times the cost of this tightly written manual."

—HERSCHELL GORDON LEWIS,
DIRECT RESPONSE WRITER/CONSULTANT/LECTURER, AND AUTHOR OF
DOZENS OF CLASSIC BOOKS ON COPY WRITING AND ADVERTISING

"Scott Bennett presents the art and science of résumé and cover letter writing in a clear, comprehensive package that will serve as a useful tool for employment seekers. I recommend his guide to all seekers and outplacement professionals."

—BARRY NEWMARK, DIRECTOR OF HUMAN RESOURCES,
BROOKLYN BUREAU OF COMMUNITY SERVICE

"It's rare to find professional wisdom and practical sense in the same book. Scott Bennett delivers both. As someone with years of experience in helping both students jump start their careers and executives choose the right applicant, I know his words can make a genuine difference at whatever step of the career ladder to which you're hoping to move."

—DR. STEVE BURGHARDT, PROFESSOR, ORGANIZATION & PLANNING,
HUNTER COLLEGE SCHOOL OF SOCIAL WORK; AND VICE-PRESIDENT, RESEARCH &
ORGANIZATIONAL DEVELOPMENT, LEADERSHIP TRANSFORMATION GROUP, LLC

"*The Elements of Résumé Style* provides a clear, well-marked path to construction of effective résumés and cover letters. It is a quick and easy read; the language and style make it inviting, and it is chock full of information essential to every level of job seeker. Usually these books are rough going and boring, but this one is supportive and fun. Young people in our Independent Living/Life Skills Program will be encouraged to use this wonderful resource as they enter the world of work."

—CAROL M. ALTOMARE, CSW, DIRECTOR,
INDEPENDENT LIVING/LIFE SKILLS PROGRAM, JEWISH CHILD CARE ASSOCIATION

"The author presents the information in such a clear, concise, well-organized way. I felt like an experienced friend was helping me through tricky territory in a very candid, yet patient and kind way."

—NINA JAFFE,
RECENT CAREER CHANGER, VERMONT

"Bennett's writing is succinct; it's a pleasure to read. His book is a delightful mix of useful, pointed, and timely content. Great help overcoming internal demons as well as external barriers. Bravo!"

—BARBARA WOOD, PH.D.,
VP FOR PATHMAKER SERVICES, GREYSTON FOUNDATION

"*The Elements of Résumé Style* is a useful addition to the literature on the art of résumé writing. It contains very detailed, specific wording recommendations not found in other books on this subject. I highly recommend it."

—ROBERT W. BLY, COPYWRITER/CONSULTANT/SEMINAR LEADER,
AND AUTHOR OF MORE THAN 50 BOOKS ON MARKETING, DIRECT MAIL,
WRITING, AND BUSINESS COMMUNICATION

The
Elements
of
Résumé
Style

The
Elements
of
Résumé
Style

ESSENTIAL RULES AND EYE-OPENING
ADVICE FOR WRITING RÉSUMÉS AND
COVER LETTERS *THAT WORK*

SCOTT BENNETT

AMACOM

American Management Association

New York • Atlanta • Brussels • Chicago • Mexico City • San Francisco
Shanghai • Tokyo • Toronto • Washington, D. C.

Special discounts on bulk quantities of AMACOM books are available to corporations, professional associations, and other organizations. For details, contact Special Sales Department, AMACOM, a division of American Management Association, 1601 Broadway, New York, NY 10019.
Tel.: 212-903-8316.   Fax: 212-903-8083.
Web site: www. amacombooks.org

This publication is designed to provide accurate and authoritative information in regard to the subject matter covered. It is sold with the understanding that the publisher is not engaged in rendering legal, accounting, or other professional service. If legal advice or other expert assistance is required, the services of a competent professional person should be sought.

ACA is a registered trademark of American Counseling Association Corp.
American Heart Association is a service mark and a registered trademark of the American Heart Association, Inc.
AMHCA is a registered trademark of American Mental Health Counseling Association.
APICS The Association for Operations Management is a registered trademark of American Production & Inventory Control Society, Inc.
Benetton is a registered trademark of Benetton Group S.P.A. Corporation Italy.
BMW is a registered trademark of BMW AG (Bayerische Motoren Werke Aktiengesellschaft).
Dale Carnegie Training is a service mark of Dale Carnegie & Associates, Inc.
Google and gmail are service marks of Google Inc.
iVillage.com is a service mark of iVillage Inc.
Kodak is a registered trademark of Eastman Kodak Company.
Microsoft, FrontPage, Hotmail, MS-DOS, PowerPoint, Visual Basic, Visual C++, Visual Interdev, Windows, and Windows NT are registered trademarks of Microsoft Corporation.
Myers-Briggs and Myers-Briggs Type Indicator are registered trademarks of Consulting Psychologists Press, Inc.
NAPM is a registered trademark of National Association of Purchasing Management.
Netscape is a service mark of Netscape Communications Corporation.
Parents' Choice is a service mark of Parents' Choice Foundation Charitable Trust.
Ping-Pong is a registered trademark of Parker Brothers, Inc.
Red Cross is a service mark of The American National Red Cross.
Salesforce.com is a registered trademark of salesforce.com, Inc.
Self-Directed Search is a registered trademark of Psychological Assessment Resources, Inc.
Sprint is a registered trademark of Sprint Communications Company L.P.
Strong Interest Inventory is a registered trademark of Stanford University Press.
The New Yorker is a registered trademark of Advance Magazine Publishers, Inc.
Tulip is a registered trademark of Duncan Enterprises Corporation.
UPS is a registered trademark of United Parcel Service of America, Inc.
YMCA is a service mark of National Council of Young Men's Christian Associations of the United States of America.

Library of Congress Cataloging-in-Publication Data

Bennett, Scott
The elements of résumé style : essential rules and eye-opening
        advice for writing résumés and cover letters that work / Scott Bennett.
    p. cm.
Includes bibliographical references and index.
ISBN-10: 0-8144-7280-X
ISBN-13: 978-0-8144-7280-4
1. Résumés (Employment) 2. Cover letters. I. Title.

HF5383.B423 2005
650.14'2—dc22

                                                          2005002842

© 2005 Scott Bennett.
All rights reserved.
Printed in the United States of America.

This publication may not be reproduced, stored in a retrieval system, or transmitted in whole or in part, in any form or by any means, electronic, mechanical, photocopying, recording, or otherwise, without the prior written permission of AMACOM, a division of American Management Association, 1601 Broadway, New York, NY 10019.

Printing number

10 9 8 7 6 5 4 3 2

This book is dedicated to

Jackie, Bonnie, and Wayne,

who share my love of words

and word-free moments, and

to every active seeker.

Contents

Introduction:
Writers Make Choices

The content of your résumé, cover letters, and other pre-interview documents is really a series of choices. This guide will provide you with an employer's perspective so you can make *informed* choices. Apply this new knowledge and you will avoid common errors, create maximum impact, and generate more responses than ever before. The choices you make as you write are crucial to generating responses. But there's more going on here.

Why Sometimes You Can Do Everything Right and Still Get No Invitation to an Interview

An error-free, clear, focused, and targeted résumé and cover letter may yield no interview for many reasons.* Here are eight:

1. As bizarre as it may sound, many organizations advertise openings already filled. Advertising such "pre-wired" jobs seems silly, but policies, contracts, or regulations often require it.

---

*However, if you've hired people yourself, you'll know the following to be true: As an employer, if you receive 200 résumés for an open position, maybe 10 are error-free (if you're lucky). The rest are discarded. Of the 10 without errors, only around five will be clear, focused, and properly targeted. These five or so folks get called for interviews. Creating an error-free, clear, focused, and targeted résumé and cover letter is within your control—and this guide will show you how to do it.

2. Some less-than-scrupulous headhunters trawl for résumés by placing an ad even when no specific position really exists, hoping to attract candidates for potential employer-clients.

3. Sudden changes (reorganizations, budget cuts, hiring freezes, or layoffs, for example) remove the need to fill an advertised opening.

4. Inefficient organizations of all sizes may take months to move from placing an ad to contacting applicants.

5. Mismatch. An employer receives enough responses from other candidates whose skills and experience are more closely suited to a specific position.

6. Timing. A well-targeted inquiry reaches an organization with suitable positions but no current openings.

7. Employer idiosyncrasies. The varied preferences of decision makers mean that the most talented candidate doesn't always prevail. For example, some hiring managers reject all graduates from certain schools. Decca Record Company rejected the Beatles in 1962 and declared, "We don't like their sound, and guitar music is on the way out."

8. Lack of civility often accounts for the absence of any response (e.g., an invitation to interview or a courtesy letter, card, or e-mail message).

Notice something in common about all these situations? The absence of an invitation to interview in such situations has absolutely nothing to do with you or your résumé or cover letter. These situations are beyond your control. Remember this, or you will mistakenly blame your résumé or cover letter or yourself for the absence of a desired response when none of these is at fault.

Pay Attention to Items Within Your Control

The trick to writing a winning résumé and cover letter is focusing carefully on the many items you *can* control.

Choose to use the tips in this guide and I believe you will increase the number of responses you receive from prospective employers. Here's why: Your compelling résumé and cover letter sent to carefully targeted readers will convey a lot about you even before any response phone call or in-person interview takes place. For example:

- You can organize data and thoughts.
- You can present complex information concisely.
- You pay attention to detail.
- You communicate in a clear and focused way.
- You are enthusiastic.
- You have useful skills.

In many ways, your résumé and cover letter are the "paper interview," and only by winning the paper interview do you have a chance at an in-person one.

Less Is More

Whenever you hear someone say, "to make a long story short," do you ever get the feeling it's too late? That ship has sailed. Again, writers make choices. I am going to encourage you repeatedly to choose your words carefully. The ability to "write short" is respected by most readers, including employers. No one is hired simply to read cover letters and résumés. Everyone who reads them has plenty of other work to do, too. If you're lucky, your documents will get eight to ten seconds of the reader's eyeball time. Direct those eyeballs carefully and use your precious few seconds of attention wisely. Respect the reader's time and you'll be ahead of most candidates.

Your résumé is not intended to list every task you performed at every position. Employers know this. I repeat: *employers know this.* It is a top-line, highlights kind of document intended to quickly give readers an honest sense of your skills, where you've been, and where you're going. It's not an autobiography. The art of the résumé is to briefly and clearly convey one's expertise and evoke enough enthusiasm from readers to get them to respond. If your résumé gets your phone to ring, it has done its job well.

Twelve Things You Can Do Without

1. Don't make stuff up. Embellishing or exaggerating the facts is the same as lying. When you don't do this, you can never get caught and you can feel better when your head hits the pillow at night.

2. Avoid automated résumé templates (i.e., "wizards" or other do-it-yourself and fill-in-the-blanks software). Résumés created using templates look like résumés created using templates. Your résumé is too important. These free or cheap tools are no replacement for time and thought. Remember: employers read many résumés. Identical formats are obvious. Different candidates will quite naturally have different résumé sections: Volunteer Experience, Language Skills, Memberships, Field Placements/Internships, and many others.

3. Avoid multiple résumés. Employers want from your résumé what you would want if you were an employer: some clear sense of where you've been, what you've done (this reveals your skills), and where you're going. One résumé provides this. Writing a different résumé for each prospective employer to "keep your options open" is a misery-making enterprise, and employers can detect the lack of direction it represents. Instead, investigate career paths of interest to you (see pp. 3–4 for ideas on how to do this) and focus on one before writing.

4. Don't load your résumé with jargon or buzzwords. Hoping

their résumés will get electronically "scanned" for "key words," some candidates insert a lot of specialized lingo. If any reader—an entry-level human resources person or any other reader who appreciates clarity—cannot understand your words, then your résumé will not evoke the responses you seek. Electronic scanners capture plenty of relevant data from résumés that are clear and accurate rather than packed with jargon. Use no mumbo jumbo.

5. If English is not your area of expertise, don't wing it. If you don't have it already, buy and read the latest edition of *The Elements of Style* by Strunk and White (only 105 pages and around eight bucks) before you write. Really!

6. Don't count on your spell-check. Spell-check is not an editor: *form* vs. *from* escapes spell-check, as does *their* vs. *there* vs. *they're*, among countless other such examples. If one mistakenly types *copletion* instead of *completion*, several versions of Microsoft Word will suggest replacing it with *copulation* instead of *completion*. Use a dictionary.

7. Don't skip the step of proofreading your finished product. In addition to rereading your documents from start to finish to check for clarity, also read them backwards to catch typos. This will slow your reading and allow you to focus on each word.

8. Don't overlook having other qualified people review your finished product. Have your documents reviewed by at least two other people (a) who routinely hire people as part of their work and (b) whose writing skills and candor you respect. Here's the hard part: listen to what they have to say. As writers, sometimes we have to delete cherished words and phrases to create the clearest, most focused documents. It often takes another qualified set of eyeballs to see what needs to be done in this regard.

9. Reject free "critiques" from résumé sellers. A critique from someone whose livelihood depends on converting the critique

into a résumé sale is not the kind of critique you need. Stick with reviewers who meet the criteria in item 8.

10. Don't broadcast ("blast") or post your résumé on the Web unless you are comfortable with (a) your co-workers or employers seeing it, (b) headhunters using it without your permission, and (c) format or content errors being sent everywhere.

11. Don't send your documents to prospective employers until you have a working answering machine or voice-mail service on every phone number that appears on your documents. Hoping that employers will call you only when you're home is folly.

12. Don't leave a silly outgoing message on your answering machine or voice mail. If you have such a message, change it to a brief, serious, audible, and clear one (without music) before you send your documents to prospective employers. Being taken seriously is crucial to your successful search.

Mindful of the foregoing, let's now address the common concerns that often—but need not—get in the way of creating an error-free, clear, focused, and targeted résumé.

The
Elements
of
Résumé
Style

1

Common Concerns

"Everyone I know has a big 'but.'"
—Pee-Wee Herman, "Pee-Wee's Big Adventure"

If you break into a cold sweat, get woozy, or just feel a little uneasy when you think about writing your résumé, then rest assured: (1) you are not alone, and (2) there is hope. Here are common concerns and guidance on each.

Are You Sure of Where You Want to Work?

Many candidates for whom the answer to this question is "no" will mistakenly send responses, inquiries, and résumés scattershot, with no clear plan. Such mailings are a waste of time because employers can detect mass mailings, broadcast faxes, and junk e-mail (spam) just as easily as the rest of us can.

You will receive few or no responses even with an error-free, clear résumé if you send it to the wrong places. Sending an otherwise excellent but poorly targeted résumé is like sending an expensive box of handmade chocolates to people with diabetes who cannot eat sweets. Effective targeting increases the response rate.

Identify and evaluate targets before you send your résumé. Ideas are all around you. Talk to friends and family members. Look at the categories from A to Z in the yellow (and blue) pages. Read ads—not only the Help Wanted ads—in daily and weekly newspapers. Leaf through the ads in the magazines you read. Listen to ads on your favorite radio stations. See ads on television. Use the Internet.*

For example, go to *click4careercoaching.com* and click on "Learn about Your Next Employer" and "Use My Great Job Links and Job Hotlines." You can use the free resources there to learn more about employers in whom you're already interested, discover new ones, and see if any are suitable targets for an inquiry letter and résumé. Doing groundwork such as this avoids the low response rates associated with inadequate targeting.

Once you have identified organizations where you might want to work, forget about whether they are hiring. Learn more about them, and if you see a potential fit (i.e., if you believe your skills and enthusiasm can add value), then send them a thoughtfully prepared inquiry letter (see pp. 63–66, 67–68) and résumé *tout de suite*.

When examining potential targets, evaluate the cultural aspects of each prospective employer. Different organizations are at different stages of existence. Consider the excitement of helping launch a start-up versus the relative stability of working in an established enterprise. Which setting do you prefer?

Similarly, the size of an organization has a big impact on the level of financial and human resources, as well as the level of structure in place. Would you rather work in a small company without bureaucracy but with few resources? Conversely, are you willing to tolerate some red tape to have more resources in place?

The operating principles of an organization permeate every aspect of work life in that organization. For example, the shared ownership of a clear mission, responsibility with authority, an unambiguous reporting structure, an environment of mutual respect, innovation, integrity at the top, and other factors impact heavily on job satisfaction.

---

*No Internet access at home? Access is free at many public libraries. Are you new to the Web? Your friendly local librarian can show you in less than two minutes how easy it is to use.

The style of an organization impacts work life, too. Dress code, work schedule, and perks (from pizza and Ping-Pong to cars, jets, and expense accounts) help shape our view of the workday and reveal a lot about an organization's view of the work ethic.

Gain insights into these and other issues from newspaper, magazine, trade journal, and Web articles, radio and television news reports, Internet message boards, employer home pages, and knowledgeable friends and family members. Doing so will allow you to make an informed selection of targets for your inquiry letter and résumé.

Well-targeted inquiry letters are so powerful that some candidates don't bother with response letters at all! These people do their reconnaissance, decide where they want to work, then methodically fax, e-mail, mail (snail-mail), and hand-deliver an inquiry letter and résumé to each target and call judiciously—not too often—to follow up until they're hired by one of the targets.

Are You Sure of What You Want to Do?

Web tools,* books, assessment instruments (e.g., Self-Directed Search, Strong Interest Inventory, Myers-Briggs Type Indicator), and other items exist to provide food for thought but not answers. View all results as suggestions, ideas, and examples—and nothing more. Only you can choose the best path for you.

Many people hesitate to choose and focus on a specific career path because they fear they may make a wrong decision. If you feel this way, be gentle with yourself. Gather information, make the most informed decision you can, then support your own decision by pursuing it with vigor. Focus on it like a laser beam.

Learn the requirements for entering the field. Are you willing to meet those requirements? If not, move on. If so, do everything in your

---

*For example, go to *click4careercoaching.com* and click on "Learn about Yourself: Match Your Interests & Skills with Careers: Play the Career Interests Game," "Learn about Many Industries: Search *U.S. Career Guide to Industries*," and "Learn about Many Types of Work: Search *U.S. Occupational Outlook Handbook*"—all free—to learn more about yourself and about potential career paths.

power to make it happen. Make the time. Ask your loved ones for understanding and support. Get the training. Apply for the student loans. Earn the certification. Pass the exams. Get the license. Find successful organizations where you can pursue your chosen path and enthusiastically target them with inquiry letters and résumés. In short, be an *active* seeker.

What if I begin working in a new career and the quality of my work isn't very good?

When we start something new, we're not supposed to be very good at it. Babies typically fall down when they first attempt to walk. We view this as normal and natural. A healthy parent praises the baby's attempts and encourages more. However, when as adults we stumble just as naturally to learn new things, we can be so very unkind to ourselves. It doesn't have to be this way. When you stumble on your new path, do a little self-parenting. Praise your efforts. Encourage yourself. And keep trying. In this spirit, the late British author Gilbert Chesterton wrote, "A thing worth doing is worth doing poorly."

What if one day I discover the choice I made is not the ideal path for me?

There is no such thing as an ideal path. We can only make the most informed choices we can make. Over time, as we establish ourselves in a new career, we naturally continue to weigh the positives and negatives of our choices, and if there is enough good stuff, we advance along the current path. If not, we investigate new paths. If instead you are frozen in place while waiting to make the perfect choice, then consider the old saying, "Perfect can be the enemy of good enough."

Any career you choose is likely not the last career you will have between now and your demise. Lighten up. Give it your best shot, and if one day you choose to change paths, congratulate yourself on your efforts, the added experience and knowledge, and move on to the next adventure.

Résumé Length

Anyone who tells you there is one hard-and-fast rule on résumé length is making it up. For obvious reasons, there is a bias among hiring managers in favor of a brief, clear, and compelling document. But this can take many forms. Many people with twenty years' work experience have a successful one-page résumé. Some people with ten years' work experience require 1¼ pages to pitch their skills most effectively. The length of your résumé depends on the nature and number of positions you have held during your unique work life.

Do you need hard-and-fast rules to follow? Here are seven:

1. As you read each word you've written, ask yourself: Does this word contribute most efficiently to the pitch? In order to save space, you may have to replace an otherwise fine word with an equally suitable shorter one. For example, *reduce* ⇨ *cut, instruct* ⇨ *train, abolish* ⇨ *end, television* ⇨ *TV, scrutinize* ⇨ *examine, information* ⇨ *data*. You get the idea.

2. As you read each action statement you've written, ask yourself: Is this information needed to make an effective pitch?

3. If the information is needed, is there a way to convey it at least as clearly using fewer words?

4. As you look at the latest draft of your résumé, ask yourself: Am I using my eight to ten seconds of each reader's attention in the most efficient way?

5. Beware of the old adage, "Material fills the available space." If you genuinely require *part* of a second page, do not interpret the blank space on page 2 as an invitation to "spread out" and write more all over your document.

6. If you require part or all of a second page, resist the urge to include a lengthy "header" (e.g., "page 2, résumé of Scott A. Bennett continued"). Instead, a simple header or footer with only your last name and the numeral 2 (e.g., *Bennett/2*) will do, if you choose to use one at all. None is needed.

7. Do not staple pages. Stapled pages make copying more difficult for recipients and the copied pages less attractive to readers.

Some candidates mistakenly believe brevity is really only for entry-level candidates. Without exception, the most effective communicators (including—it's no coincidence—most senior-level candidates) tend to create brief résumés. The ability to communicate effectively is prized by every employer. Show employers you possess this skill by "writing short." Candidates who "write long" reveal (1) an inability to organize and convey complex information quickly and (2) disrespect for the reader's time.

A résumé is not a *curriculum vitae* (CV). A CV is generally used by academics and tends to be longer than a résumé. It includes more detailed chronologies of presentations, publications, field, teaching, and research experiences and more, and can run many pages. Such length and detail is inappropriate for a résumé. By applying the tips in this guide, anyone wishing to do so can convert a CV into a clear, focused, and compelling résumé.

Chronological or Functional Résumé?

Use reverse-chronological (newest to oldest) format. Most employers prefer it because it's more direct and easier to read. Plus, employers are already in on the much-touted "secret": functional (nonchronological) résumés are used to disguise a work history the candidate thinks needs disguising. Is this a message you want to send?

Use reverse-chronological format for any sections with chronological entries (e.g., Work Experience; Field Placements/Internships; Volunteer Experience; Education; Inventions, Published Works, Seminars).

Employment Gaps

Real people often have gaps in their work histories. Don't hide gaps by extending exit dates or pushing up start dates on your résumé. People get laid off or fired. We care for children or other loved ones. We recover from illnesses, traumas, or injuries. We serve time for crimes. We go to school. We do countless other things as we move through life. All such gaps can be explained in an interview. If a hiring manager reads the résumé of an obviously skilled person with a lengthy gap, he or she will simply ask the candidate about it, not burn the résumé. Be kind to yourself on this point, and focus on clearly showing (through position descriptions, volunteer experience, software skills, language skills, etc.) the transferable skills you can bring to your next employer.

Re-entry after an extended gap is achievable. If you can keep up with relevant trade journals or take continuing education courses during the gap, great. It's not required, though. If, for example, while working in purchasing you were able to establish vendor relationships once (or, say, working in public relations you were able to establish media relationships once), remember: you obviously have the skills to do it again.

A few recruiters insist that gaps are unacceptable. These few are not among the smartest in their field. Being ruled out for a position on the basis of a gap is a useful warning. You wouldn't want to work for them, anyway.

Include Interim Jobs?

A vice-president laid off from a manufacturing firm tends bar while looking for a suitable new position. A marketing director fired from a media company cleans houses while he searches for another marketing position. A controller whose Internet firm closed takes bookkeeping assignments from a temp agency until she finds her next permanent job. Should these interim jobs be part of their résumés?

This is a decision each candidate must make.* If positions you view as interim jobs are included on your résumé, some readers will

---

*When completing a public-sector (government) employment application (frequently required in lieu of or in addition to a résumé), the choice is clearer: usually, omission of any position is a violation of law.

respect your work ethic and honesty. Some may exploit the information by offering a lower salary. Still others may do both.

Don't assume the worst, however. Let's say the salary range in your area for the position you seek is $60,000–$80,000. It is the rare hiring manager who will ignore the range and try to get your services for $40,000 just because he or she estimates you're earning half that much at an interim job. Yes, private-sector employers (except nonprofits, which often can't afford to pay as much, anyway) exist to maximize profits, and this includes cutting costs, but they must also compete in the marketplace to attract and *retain* qualified staff. Getting you for a few months "on the cheap," then quickly losing you to another better-paying employer is no bargain.

If you decide to omit interim jobs from your résumé, then adhere to the spirit of truth-in-advertising: Change the Work Experience section heading to Relevant Work Experience.

Self-Employment

Include self-employment as you would include any other position. Do not make up inflated titles like "Chief Executive Officer" or "Chairman of the Board" for your role in a solo operation.

> 5/96–present   Self-employed, Metropolis, NY
>   Freelance Writer and Lecturer
> [3- to 6-sentence position description/blurb here...]
> [Strike TAB key after *present* on first line and at beginning of second line.]

Many former entrepreneurs mistakenly fear that prospective employers will view them as (1) unwilling or unable to report to others and (2) failures. The first of these fears is groundless and the second is impossible. First, former entrepreneurs have been where the buck stops. They understand—perhaps more clearly than other employees—the need to quickly pitch in and get something done without endless debate. Second, while a business can be a failure, a person cannot be a failure. People don't turn into goats after a business fails. They're still successes as people.

The accomplishments of entrepreneurs (especially the lessons learned) add value to their candidacies. Such candidates are usually (by necessity) excellent multitaskers and proficient at managing limited resources. Most employers also recognize the determination and intensity required to launch any enterprise.

Job Hopping

Why do candidates who perceive themselves as job hoppers seek résumé-writing advice? What's the one thing we know for sure about job hoppers, even before we meet them? They are already clever at getting jobs. Perhaps they are falsifying or omitting start and exit dates or using a nonchronological résumé format in an attempt to camouflage reality. Some may present real dates on a reverse-chronological format. All are convincing explainers.

Although few agree on a precise definition for "job hopper," if you view yourself as one, then employers may, too. However, a couple of hops does not a bunny make. If, for example, after one year in a job you were laid off, then worked six months, then left to care for a loved one who suddenly fell ill, this is not hopping. Hopping is a continuing pattern over many years.

Even such patterns are increasingly accepted in many fields, especially if you added value at each organization and learned new skills or lessons from each experience. Interestingly, more and more candidates find it helpful to think of themselves like ballplayers or coaches, adding value and then moving from place to place within one career path or industry as the market dictates.

If over many years you hop from job to job, dissatisfied and with no obvious game plan, you can choose now to shift from disguising reality to improving it. Listen to the message your job hopping may be sending you and choose to act on it:

- Do you need to explore organizations and career paths with requirements more closely suited to your skills, interests, and values? If so, turn to pages 1–4 for ideas on how to do this.
- Do you leave jobs in anger? If so, buy and read *How to Control Your Anger Before It Controls You* by Albert Ellis and Raymond Chip Tafrate (New York: Citadel Press, 1997).

Next, we'll look beyond words and phrases to the nonobvious yet powerful presentation elements of a winning résumé.

2

Presentation:
The Reader Sees
More than Words

Just as your unspoken communications (e.g., facial expressions, wardrobe) often set the tone for your spoken words and deeply affect how those words are received, there are a number of elements beyond the words in your résumé that set the tone for your written words and have great impact on the reader's level of interest and attention. Here they are.

Paper

So many candidates use nonwhite paper these days that you will probably attract more attention with white paper. If you can afford it, fluorescent white 24-pound 100 percent cotton is ideal (e.g., search for item number 20288 at *www.crane.com*). If not, regular bright white 24-pound bond will suffice. The choice you make here is a lot like the modest investment that home sellers make to improve the curb appeal of their home—such an investment is usually money well spent.

Ink

Print your résumé in black, the most suitable color for those and other pre-interview documents. If you use inks other than black, you risk not being taken seriously by employers.

Unfortunately, each time you type an e-mail address, many versions of Microsoft Word (and some other word processing software) automatically underline it and change its color from black to blue. The result inappropriately draws the reader's attention away from your name, the most important item at the top of each document. Thus, it is important to remove both the underline and the blue type from your e-mail address on each document. (You need to do this even if you have only a black-and-white printer, because when you attach your documents to an e-mail message—more on this later—the recipient will see that underline and blue print.) Here's how to do that:

1. Block (SHIFT-⇨) the e-mail address.
2. Go to Format and select Font.
3. Select Underline: (none).
4. Select Color: Black.
5. Click OK.
6. Click ⇩ to unblock text.

Margins

Set all margins (left and right, top and bottom) to 1 inch. Resist the temptation to make the margins smaller than this in order to cram more text onto a page. Instead, use fewer words and choose each word carefully. Maintaining 1 inch margins will help your résumé stand out from the stack.

Spacing

After each sentence, strike the space bar only once. Some people strike it twice, and over the course of a page, this wastes a lot of valuable space.

Use tabs for uniform appearance. For example:

1/99–1/02	Big Giant Company, Inc., Metropolis, NY
12/00–1/02	Director, Client Service
[3- to 6-sentence position description/blurb here…]	
6/00–12/00	Client Service Supervisor
1/99–6/00	Client Service Representative

After the date and before the name of the employer, strike the TAB key, not multiple spaces. The same applies between each end date and job title. Doing so will avoid your having to play with the space bar in the hopes of eventually lining up text evenly.

If you find your text flowing onto a second page by only a few lines, here are two ways you can create extra space on the first page instead:

1. Take advantage of an optical illusion: an 8-point blank line looks a lot like the space of a regular text line. Thus, change every blank line on page 1 to 8-point type. For each blank line (each line with no text), move the cursor to the beginning of the line, SHIFT-⇨, then change the font size to 8 point. After doing this for all the blank lines, you may see your overflow text pop back onto page 1.

2. Adjust the space between characters. This is called "kerning." Here is an example:

> Use kerning if and only if there is slight spillover to a second page. [normal kerning]
>
> Use kerning if and only if there is slight spillover to a second page. [kerning condensed 0.2 point]

See the difference? It may seem minor, but over an entire document, the space savings are considerable. Here's how to do it:

1. Move the cursor to the beginning of your document.

2. Block (SHIFT-⇩) all text.

3. Click on Format and select Font.

4. Select Character Spacing.

5. Under Spacing, select Condense and select By 0.2 point.

6. Click OK.

7. Click ⇩ to unblock text.

If you use kerning, (1) use it for the entire document, not just select words or phrases, and (2) condense by no more than 0.2 point or the result will look ridiculous. Really it will.

Type the sections directly below their headings. Some candidates mistakenly waste one-third of the page by typing all the content to the right of each heading:

Work Experience 1/99–1/02   Big Giant Company, Metropolis, NY
12/00–1/02 Director, Client Service
[3- to 6-sentence position description/blurb
here…]
6/00–12/00 Client Service Supervisor
1/99–6/00   Client Service Representative

This is a waste of space. Instead, stick with the following:

Work Experience

1/99–1/02   Big Giant Company, Inc., Metropolis, NY
12/00–1/02   Director, Client Service
[3- to 6-sentence position description/blurb here…]
6/00–12/00   Client Service Supervisor
1/99–6/00   Client Service Representative

Although the first example may appear to use less space than the second example, it actually uses more once the position descriptions/blurbs are in place. The suggested format (the second example) uses space much more efficiently and still leaves plenty of room on both sides for readers to scribble comments or questions.

Font

Select a serif font (like Times New Roman) for your documents. Research conducted by many print advertising experts has proved such fonts are easier for readers to understand* and thus generate more responses than **sans-serif (flat)** fonts. It is tempting to play "fun with fonts," but instead stick with what is proven to work.

☹ **What if the Hokey-Pokey really is what it's all about?**
[Arial, a sans-serif font, proven to generate fewer responses]

☹ **What if the Hokey-Pokey really is what it's all about?**
[Univers, a sans-serif font, proven to generate fewer responses]

☺ What if the Hokey-Pokey really is what it's all about?
[Times New Roman, a serif font, proven to generate more responses]

Playing "Fun with Fonts"

Some folks mistakenly think that using bullets, lots of different **fonts**, **bold**, *italics*, ALL CAPS, <u>underlining</u>, and silly ***combinations of*** THESE will get a reader's attention. The truth is, when we accentuate everything (or too much), we accentuate nothing. Candidates often ask, "If I don't use these tricks, what will get their attention?" Your content (i.e., your properly positioned examples of transferable skills) will get their attention. Content sells.

Font Size

Use no more than two font sizes to avoid a carnival-like, disorganized appearance. Use one size for your name (16 or 18 point), and another for the rest (11 or 12 point).

Resist the temptation to use smaller font sizes in order to cram more text onto a page. Again, instead use fewer words and choose each word carefully.

---

*Tony Antin, *Great Print Advertising: Creative Approaches, Strategies, and Tactics* (New York: John Wiley & Sons, 1993), pp. 125–126.

Boldface

Apply **boldface** only to your name and the section headings. This will provide readers with an easy path through your information. Resist the temptation to apply **boldface** to anything else.

Italics

Use *italics* only for the names of publications (e.g., *The New Yorker*) and foreign phrases, if any (e.g., *cum laude* to express "with honors").

All Caps

Don't use ALL CAPS on your résumé. They serve no constructive purpose, and many readers interpret their use as rude (i.e., the written equivalent of shouting).

Underlining

Don't use <u>underlining</u> on your résumé. Like ALL CAPS, <u>underlining</u> draws the reader's eyes away from parts of your résumé. Is there any part of your résumé from which you want the reader to look away?

Now that you have the tools you need to help you set the tone for your words, we'll explore how even items as simple as contact information send messages to the reader.

3

Even the Simplest Items Send Messages to the Reader

Like in many realms of life, little things mean a lot on your résumé, too.

Your Name

If your name ends in "Jr." or "II" or "III" or "IV" and so on, you may choose to omit such designation from your résumé. When these designations are used, readers may perceive you as defining yourself largely in terms of your relationship to someone else, and this may be viewed less favorably in the United States than in other countries. If you share a phone number with another person whose identity is frequently confused with yours, you're in a tough spot and you may have to include the designation. Avoid it if you can.

Do not attempt to disguise your gender or ethnicity (or the appearance of a particular ethnicity) by using initials instead of names. However, if you are really called by your initials, then place them in quotes and in parentheses:

Julio ("J.T.") Bennett

Omit academic degrees (e.g., AA, AS, BA, BFA, BS, DDS, DO, DVM, EdD, JD, MA, MBA, MD, MFA, MLS, MS, MSW, PhD) from your name on the résumé. Your identity and your training are two different things. There's a home for this information in the Education section. Avoid duplication.

Your Address

If you live in an apartment, include your apartment number on your résumé. Many candidates mistakenly think a house address appears more prestigious than an apartment address, so they omit this information. However, mail is easily delayed or lost when the apartment number is missing, so include it in your address.

If you can, avoid using a post office box for an address. It implies instability and impermanence to the reader.

Do not spell out the name of your state. Use the generally accepted two-letter capitalized postal abbreviation. You have at most ten seconds of your reader's eyeball time. Don't waste a second on trivia.

If you do not know it already, get your nine-digit Zip code from *www.usps.com* or from your local post office. Using it is a sign that you pay attention to detail, a valued skill.

Your Phone Number

Include your home and/or personal cell phone number. Not your work phone. Not a cell phone paid for by your employer. Callers can generally infer from the voice-mail message on an employer-paid phone that it is an employer-paid phone. You do not want to be perceived as someone who uses—and will use—an employer's time and resources to find another job.

Do not include pager numbers of any kind, business or personal. Make responding easy for the reader.

Your Fax Number

If you have a home fax number, list it. Do not use an employer's fax number.

Your E-Mail Address

An e-mail address implies comfort with computers. If you have a personal e-mail address you check daily, then list it. If not, do not. If your personal e-mail address is silly, create a new and more appropriate one. (At the time of this writing, free e-mail is available at *www.gmail.com, www.yahoo.com, www.hotmail.com,* and other sites.) In order to be contacted, you must first be taken seriously. Use this new e-mail address for sending résumés to prospective employers and check it for new mail daily. Do not send from one address and ask recipients to respond to—by having to type or cut and paste—another address. Again, make responding easy for the reader.

The more attention you give to such details, the less work you ask your reader to do. When reading résumés, hiring managers sometimes feel like the Rodney Dangerfields of the work world: they get no respect. Be the exception; sweat the details and respect your reader.

4

Sell Your Skills and Experience—Always with the Reader in Mind

We all long to be understood. Yet we know in life that a message received is often very different from the message sent. As you craft every section of your résumé, think about the receiver of your sales message so that your skills and experience—your unique story—can be easily and rapidly understood.

Goal Section?

The only people who need a Goal section on their résumés are those who are changing careers. If you are not changing careers, do not include a Goal section. If you are changing careers, then give the goal a lot of thought because this (brief!) item must clearly state your intent to transition from your past work experience to your desired work experience.

A goal statement need not exceed two sentences. Keep in mind: transferable skills are what matter, and those will be clear from your position descriptions/blurbs and other sections. Keep your goal statement brief. For example, "Transition to and establish career in X." may serve as a suitable goal statement.

Avoid a common error: do not use "To" as the first word in a goal. Instead, begin every sentence on your résumé, including your goal (if you need one), with a verb/action word.

Goal vs. Objective

Both "goal" and "objective" convey the same information, but the latter takes longer to read. *Goal* conveys the needed information and respects the reader's time.

Executive Summary Section?

A summary at the top of a résumé is often interpreted to mean, "My résumé is kind of long and tedious. Here is the good stuff you really need to know about me, so you need not actually read the whole document." Is this an admission you want to make? Properly written, your résumé *is* a summary. If it needs summarizing, then it needs work.

Give Readers a Reason to Believe

Despite our best intentions, sometimes our wording is too vague to be taken seriously—and in the absence of clear evidence, vague claims are usually interpreted as empty claims.

Most of the résumés employers receive are loaded with vague claims. Avoid such claims and your résumé will stand out from the stack. See examples in Figure 1.

Figure 1. Vague claims to avoid.

Able	Appealing	Capable
Active	Articulate*	Careful
Adaptable	Assertive	Cautious
Adept	Astute	Charitable
Aggressive	Attentive	Charming
Alert*	Attractive	Cheerful
Amazing	Brilliant	Clean*
Ambitious	Bubbly	Clear-headed
Amiable	Business-like	Clever
Analytical	Calm*	Committed*

Compassionate

Competent

Competitive

Confident

Conscientious

Conservative

Consistent

Cool-headed

Cooperative

Courageous

Courteous

Creative

Curious

Customer-oriented

Daring

Decisive

Dedicated*

Dependable

Detail-minded

Detail-oriented

Determined*

Diligent

Diplomatic

Disciplined*

Discreet

Eager

Easy-going

Effective

Effervescent

Efficient

Energetic

Enterprising

Enthusiastic

Ethical

Excellent

Experienced*

Extrovert

Fabulous

Fair

Fantastic

Firm*

Flexible

Forceful

Frank

Friendly

Generous

Goal-oriented

Gregarious

Hands-on

Hard-working

Healthy

Helpful

High-energy

Honest

Humble

Humorous

Imaginative

Independent

Industrious

Innovative

Instrumental

Introspective

Introvert

Judicious

Kind

Knowledgeable

Level-headed

Logical

Loving

Loyal

Mature

Methodical

Meticulous

Modest

Motivated*

Multi-tasking

Neat

Objective

Obliging

Open-minded

Optimistic

Organized*

Original

Outgoing

Patient*

People person

People-oriented

Perceptive

Persevering

Persistent

Personable

Persuasive

Pleasant

(continues)

Figure 1. (*continued*).

Poised	Savvy	Successful
Positive	Seasoned*	Supportive
Practical	Self-confident	Swell
Proactive	Self-managing	Tactful
Productive	Self-motivated	Takes initiative
Professional	Self-reliant	Talented
Proficient	Self-starter	Team player
Receptive	Sense of humor	Tenacious
Reliable	Sensitive	Vivacious
Resilient	Sharp	Well-groomed
Resourceful	Sincere	Well-organized
Responsible	Sophisticated	Wonderful
Results-driven	Spectacular	Zestful
Results-oriented	Strong	Zippy
Sassy	Suave	

*Do not use as an adjective/descriptive word.

Why write such vague and unconvincing claims when specific action statements provide quick and powerful evidence of important skills? For example, compare "Excellent written communications skills" and "Wrote jargon-free *User Guide* for 11,000 users." Do you see the crucial difference? The former is hollow self-puffery; the latter, credible evidence of a useful skill. See Figure 2 for more examples.

As you write:

- Avoid vague claims.
- Use brief, specific examples to demonstrate—rather than merely claim—skills.

Figure 2. Hollow self-puffery versus evidence of useful skills.

Vague Claims, Viewed by Readers as Hollow Self-Puffery	Specific Action Statements, Viewed by Readers as Evidence of Useful Skills
Experience working in fast-paced environment.	Registered 120+ third-shift emergency room patients/night.
Excellent verbal skills.	Trained 30 new hires on customer service protocols.
Confident and poised.	Developed and presented cost-reduction plan to board of directors.
Team player with cross-functional awareness.	Collaborated with clients, A/R, and Sales to increase speed of receivables and prevent interruption of service to clients.
Rare combination of superior interpersonal skills and in-depth technical skills understanding.	Translated complex changes into jargon-free written updates for nontechnical users in 4 countries.
Provided a broad-based flow of data.	Interpreted survey results to create 16 unique monthly reports for Sales, Marketing, and Finance.
Dedicated hands-on management style.	Cut annual employee turnover rate 85% (from 40%/year to 6%/year) in 36 months.

(continues)

Figure 2. *(continued)*.

Vague Claims, Viewed by Readers as Hollow Self-Puffery	Specific Action Statements, Viewed by Readers as Evidence of Useful Skills
Demonstrated success in analyzing client needs.	Created and implemented comprehensive needs assessment mechanism to help forecast demand for services and staffing.
Make well-thought-out decisions.	Created RFPs with clear requirements, evaluated complex results, and selected new suppliers.

Education or Work Experience Section First?

If you are attending or you recently completed vocational school, college, or graduate school, and you have little relevant work experience, place your Education section first. If you have a lot of relevant work experience (even if you recently returned to school), place your Work Experience section first.

"Work Experience" vs. "Professional Experience"

Both terms convey the same information, but the latter takes longer to read. "Work Experience" conveys the needed information and respects the reader's time.

"Experience" alone (without "Work" or "Professional") is ideal, but only on résumés with no Volunteer Experience section.

No colon is required after this or any other section heading on your résumé.

Position Descriptions/Blurbs

When the starting month and year and ending month and year are omitted from an entry, readers may infer: (1) an attempt to disguise gaps (whether the candidate is doing so or not), (2) the candidate has a poor memory, or (3) the candidate is too lazy to retrieve the information. None of these is a desirable message to send. Include the starting month and year and ending month and year for each entry.

In the United States, there is no zero used to express any of the months, except in "10" to represent October. For example, "January 2003 through July 2005" is written "1/03–7/05," not "01/03–07/05," and not "January 2003 through July 2005"—also a waste of the reader's time.

Omit the street addresses and Zip codes of employers. The city and state will do:

1/99–1/02	Big Giant Company, Inc., Metropolis, NY
[Strike TAB key after end date.]	

Think outside the cubicle: replace "internal-speak" position titles with titles outsiders can easily understand. If, for example, your internal title is CSR4, then write an accurate and understandable equivalent instead (e.g., Senior Customer Service Representative). Make understanding easy for the reader.

Exclude bullets. Long ago, bullets were intended to precede a single word. Over time people stretched their use to phrases, then whole thoughts, then paragraphs with connecting thoughts. Nowadays, bullets waste space on a résumé. Neither a bullet nor any other symbol will propel a reader's eyes and interest on a résumé as quickly as a thoughtful and succinct paragraph. Use from three to six sentences/action statements in a paragraph to construct a position description/blurb for each position.

On an 8½ x 11-inch résumé page with 1-inch margins, a position description/blurb as long as the preceding paragraph would (1) save space and (2) require readers to move their eyes from left to right five times. This is faster and easier—37.5 percent fewer eye movements—than reading the same words with bullets. Look at the points made in the previous paragraph, presented instead in a bulleted list:

- Exclude bullets.

- Long ago, bullets were intended to precede a single word. Over time people stretched their use to phrases, then whole thoughts, then paragraphs with connecting thoughts.

- Nowadays, bullets waste space on a résumé.

- Neither a bullet nor any other symbol will propel a reader's eyes and interest on a résumé as quickly as a thoughtful and succinct paragraph.

- Use from three to six sentences/action statements in a paragraph to construct a position description/blurb for each position.

On an 8½ x 11-inch résumé page with 1-inch margins, a position description as long as the preceding bulleted list would (1) waste space and (2) require readers to move their eyes from left to right eight times. This is slower and more difficult—60 percent more eye movements—than reading the same words in a paragraph. Make understanding easy for the reader and make the most effective use of your eight to ten seconds of the reader's attention—use thoughtful and succinct paragraphs for position descriptions.

Some positions, especially the more junior or less recent ones with obvious titles, require no descriptive blurb at all. Every reader knows what a cashier or a waiter does, for example. There's no need to list each task.

If you held the same position in two or more organizations, just one descriptive blurb may be required. There are exceptions, however; each case is unique. For example, a candidate who has worked as an emergency room nurse at three urban public hospitals may require only one blurb, while a candidate who has worked as an emergency room nurse at one tribal hospital, one suburban private hospital, and one urban public hospital may require three blurbs.

When writing about positions assigned through a temporary agency, candidates often mistakenly list their work sites as their employers. Doing this is not only inaccurate but also may later be seen as an attempt to intentionally misrepresent the facts. Your employer is the organization that issues your payroll checks; this is usually the agency. Work sites are appropriately named in the blurb, especially if they are particularly prestigious.

Exclude the word *I* from your résumé. Start every sentence with a verb/action word (see Figure 5). Remember to include cooperative verbs, too. For example, "Co-created X," "Participated in development of X," "Collaborated with A and B on X," and like phrases tell employers you play well with others.

Look beyond the usual for the strongest and most accurate action words. Some examples from the list shown in Figure 5 (presented later) are: *adapt, analyze, cultivate, defuse, enhance, familiarize, foster, harness, initiate, interpret, navigate, nurture, persuade, streamline, synthesize, and target.* Use present-tense verbs (e.g., *write*) as appropriate for your current position and past-tense verbs (e.g., *wrote*) for all previous positions.

Save space:

- Although in other documents the numbers 1 through 9 are often expressed in words, in résumé blurbs these numbers may be expressed using numerals (e.g., 1, 2, 3...) instead.
- The numbers 10 and up may be expressed using numerals as well (e.g., 40; 800; 12,000).
- When referring to monetary values, use *K* to express "thousands" (e.g., $20K instead of $20,000, $20 thousand, 20 thousand dollars, or twenty thousand dollars).
- When referring to monetary values, use *M* to express "millions" (e.g., $20M instead of $20,000,000, $20 million, 20 million dollars, or twenty million dollars).

- The phrase "more than" may be expressed by adding a plus (+) to a number (e.g., "Wrote *XYZ Quarterly* for 500+ staff" instead of "Wrote *XYZ Quarterly* for more than 500 staff").

- The word *percent* may be expressed using the symbol (%) instead (e.g., "Achieved record-setting 117% of annual sales quota").

- The word *per* may be replaced with the forward slash (/) (e.g., "Achieved fivefold sales increase—from $120K to $720K/year").

- If necessary, the word *and* may also be expressed using the forward slash (/) (e.g., "Analyzed 50 businesses owned/operated by consumers with mental illnesses").

More Words and Phrases to Avoid

Why write "utilize" when "use" is simpler and more direct? Why write "Was responsible for office management" when "Managed office" is more active and more direct?

If *any* of the words or phrases in Figure 3 are on your résumé, then cut them out and rewrite your sentences so they are simpler and more direct.

Figure 3. More words and phrases to avoid.

A	Are	Basically
Accompany (use *escort*)	Ascertain (use *discover* or *learn* or *determine*)	Because
Accumulate		Benchmark
Actually	Assume	Best practice
Add value	At the present time (use *now*)	Big picture
Am		Blaze
Ameliorate (use *improve*)	Avoid (use *avert*)	Bleeding edge
An	B to B	Brainstorm
Appease	Ball park	Broad-based
Architect (as a verb)	Bandwidth	Business logic
		Buy in

Carry out

Catalyst

Cease (use *stop* or *end*)

Challenge

Charge

Client-focused

Clone (unless you are in science)

Command

Commence

Competency

Concerning (use *on* or *about*)

Conciliate (use *reconcile*)

Consequently

Constitute (use *form*)

Core

Countless

Cross-functional

Currently (use *now*)

Cutting edge

Cycle

Deal (as a verb)

Decrease (use *cut*)

Deliverable

Dialogue (as a verb)

Disincent (not a word)

Dissect (unless you are in science, use *examine*)

Disseminate (use

publish or *send out*)

Downsize

Dream

Drill down

Due to the fact that

Duties

Economize

Ecosystem

Effectuate

Empower

Empowering

Empowerment

Endeavor

End result

Excellence

Fast-track

Figure (as a verb; use *calculate*)

Final outcome

Fine-tune

Fire (as a verb; use *dismiss* or *replace*)

Float (as a verb)

Following (use *after*)

For the purpose of (use *for*)

Fortify (use *strengthen*)

Front line

Function (as a verb; use *serve*)

Functionality

Game plan

Gap analysis

Globalization

Going forward

Go public

Group (as a verb)

Guarantee (as a verb)

Hardball

Harmonize (unless you are in music)

Harvest (unless you are in farming/science)

Head (use *lead*)

Her

High level

His

I

In reference to

In the event that (use *if*)

In the loop

Incent (not a word)

Indeed

In-depth study

Indicate

Interact

Interface (as a verb)

Interpersonal

Interrelated

(continues)

Figure 3. (*continued*).

Is

Just

Keep (use *retain*)

Keynote (as a verb)

Knowledge base

Leadership

Leading edge

Leverage

Little

Lower (use *cut* or *reduce*)

Manipulate

Many

Me

Memorize

Mindset

Mine

Mission

Mitigate (use *ease*)

Moreover

Move the ball

Moving forward

My

Myriad

Necessitate

Numerous

Objective (use *goal*)

Off-line

Off-site

Orientate (use *orient*)

Our

Outline (as a verb; use *summarize*)

Out of the loop

Out-of-pocket

Outside the box

Oversee (use *supervise* or *manage*)

Paradigm

Parameter

Paramount

Particularly

Past experience

Perfect (as a verb or an adjective)

Peruse (use *review*)

Point in time

Possess (use *own*)

Possibility

Preplan (unless you are in the fire service; otherwise, use *plan*)

Preventative (use *preventive*)

Proactively

Problem-solve

Prototype (as a verb)

Quality-driven

Quite

Really

Rectify (use *correct* or

amend)

Regarding (use *on* or *about*)

Reinforce

Remainder (unless you are in publishing)

Remediate

Remember

Remunerate (use *compensate* or *pay*)

Repeat

Responsibilities

Responsible for

Re-vision

Revisit

Right-size

Schema

School (as a verb; use *educate* or *train*)

Scope (as a verb)

Set up

Simulate

Smart-size

So

Solutions

Spearhead (use *initiate* or *lead*)

Spell out

State-of-the-art

Strategize (use *plan*)

Subsequently	Tolerate	Viable
Substantiate (use *prove* or *verify*)	Touch base	Viable alternative
	Totally	Virtual
Such	Total quality	Vision (as a verb)
Suggest (use *propose*)	Transpire	Visioning
	Undertake	Visualize
Target audience	Underwrite (use *sponsor*)	Was
Team (as a verb)		Well
Team building	Until such time as (use *until*)	Were
That		Which
The	Utilize (use *use*)	Win-win
There	Value-added	World-class
This	Verbalize	www
Thought leader	Verbally	
Time frame	Very	

The blurb is not intended to list everything you did in each position. Employers know this. I repeat: *employers know this.* Be terse and pithy. Get to the point. Stick to the highlights. A descriptive blurb is not a job description. In fact, if you are using a copy of a job description to help you write your résumé, throw it away. Instead, as you write a blurb for each position, think beyond your specific tasks and your department:

- In what ways does your work impact other departments?
- In what ways does your work contribute to the overall success of the organization?
- Have you identified problems and solved them? If so, give brief examples.
- Have you identified opportunities and acted on them? If so, give brief examples.

- Have you worked collaboratively? If so, what did doing so accomplish?

- Pretend you're the reader. As an employer, what would you want to know?

What's your "elevator speech"? If you ran into a prospective employer in an elevator, how would you describe the highlights of what you do in three or four concise sentences, before the elevator arrives at the employer's floor? Think about it. Once you've figured this out, drop the word *I* from each sentence and, *voilà*, you have the blurb for your present position.

Sample Position Descriptions/Blurbs

1/00–present   click4careercoaching.com, Metropolis, NY
               General Manager (part-time)
Provide free career resources. Write articles on résumé writing and interview skills. Select for inclusion useful information (sites, books, and software) on self-assessment, career exploration, salary negotiation, self-employment, education, and jobs (for-profit, public, and nonprofit).

Do not justify (even lines on right-hand side) the blurbs. An aligned left edge with a ragged right edge is much easier to read.

9/00–3/01   XYZ Foundation, Metropolis, NY
               Career Developer
Provided comprehensive career counseling to staff at all levels and to clients, including formerly homeless, ex-offenders, persons living with HIV/AIDS/mental illness, recovering from substance abuse, and moving from welfare to work. Compiled and distributed job data and resources related to literacy, learning disabilities, credit counseling, driver training, job preparedness, and vocational training. Launched JobLand career counseling office.

11/97–5/99   ABC College School of Business, Metropolis, NY
                   Career Services Counselor
Launched Career Services Office. Facilitated workshops for and
counseled 2,000+ students and alumni on résumés, cover letters,
pre-interview research, interviews, and post-interview follow-up
skills. Developed mailings, broadcast faxes, job bank, job search
training materials, and annual résumé book.

4/92–4/96   Public Service Computer Software, Metropolis, MA
8/94–4/96   President and Chief Operating Officer
Published country's best-selling administrative and educational
software for firefighters. Published three educational software titles
for kids 11 and older: *UpFront Sex, Drugs, and Rock & Roll* (awarded
Parents' Choice Honors), *UpFront Geography: You Can't Get There
From Here*, and *UpFront History: What'd That Dead Guy Do?*
6/93–8/94   Sales and Marketing VP
Expanded number of users from 2,000 to 11,000+. Collaborated
with technical team to meet complex and frequently changing local,
state, and federal client specifications.
4/92–6/93   Sales Manager

Notice that there is no blurb for Sales Manager. A blurb is not always required for every position. In this case, the blurb for Sales and Marketing VP conveys an overview of sales achievement.

Notice also that present-tense verbs/action words are used for a current position and past-tense verbs/action words for past positions.

On an 8½ x 11-inch résumé page with 1-inch margins, none of the sample blurbs uses more than six lines of text—the most that's needed to convey the highlights of nearly any position. See Appendix A for more examples of effective position descriptions/blurbs.

Sentences/Action Statements

The action statements in each blurb represent examples of the skills you can bring to bear wherever you work. The power of these examples is at the heart of a winning résumé. Make each action statement clear, pack it with compelling evidence of your relevant skills, and keep it brief. See Figure 4.

(text continues on page 38)

Figure 4. Sentences/action statements.

- Achieved $X in weekly sales.
- Achieved sixfold sales increase—from $120K to $840K/year.
- Co-chaired Continuous Quality Improvement Team.
- Co-developed system to streamline O and P.
- Collaborated with materials vendors to cut lead times in half. (The phrase "in half" is more quickly read than "by 50%." Similarly, for example, "tripled" is a quicker and more powerful read than "increased by 200%.")
- Completed M ahead of deadline and under budget.
- Conducted disaster-recovery training for X staff.
- Cut average accounts receivable from 62 to 38 days.
- Cut monthly expenses X% to $X.
- Defined and implemented procedures to serve E, F, and G.
- Defused tensions and promoted collaboration among sales and market research staffs, yielding faster, more relevant research.
- Designed recruitment literature and managed its production and distribution.
- Doubled monthly sales to $X.
- Evaluated and recommended J.
- Evaluated and selected K.
- Extracted relevant data from H to create timely I.
- Fostered collaboration among W, X, and Y to increase Z.
- Identified prospects. Closed $X in new business in first year.
- Increased annual sales X% to $X.
- Initiated and developed procedures to accelerate communication among L, M, and N.
- Initiated and implemented outsourcing of payroll, reducing administrative costs by $X/year.
- Introduced and enforced protocols for B, C, and D.
- Managed $X annual budget.
- Managed high volume of I.
- Managed introduction, pricing, promotion, and branding of Q.
- Managed migration of U system from mainframe to client/server environment.
- Managed relationships with D, E, and F.

- Managed X staff.
- Met complex local, state, and federal requirements.
- Met time-sensitive requirements of G and H.
- Nurtured small business clients, moving several from under $X to more than $Y/year.
- Participated in development of A.
- Performed outreach to J and K.
- Persuaded colleagues at corporate headquarters to replace retiring domestic fleet vehicles with more fuel-efficient imports, saving $X/year.
- Persuaded R and S to collaborate on new T strategy.
- Produced content for, maintained, and marketed X websites.
- Provided seamless transition to successor.
- Quadrupled annual sales to $X.
- Recruited, extensively trained, and remotely supervised X.
- Reduced expenses $X/year.
- Scrutinized expense reports to identify errors. Trained staff on proper expense reporting to prevent recurrences.
- Selected sites and managed complex logistics for X trade shows.
- Served as liaison among V, W, and Y to develop Z.
- Streamlined in-house recruiting function, reducing average vacancy time frame by 14 days.
- Successfully integrated two culturally disparate sales forces and streamlined processes, resulting in X% margin increases and smaller staff able to serve X% more customers.
- Synthesized survey results from multiple sources to develop clear system requirements.
- Thrived amid X mergers/acquisitions. (Instead of explaining complex ownership and organizational changes, this brief sentence lets readers easily infer your flexibility and relationship skills.)
- Trained X staff on service protocols and quality measurement.
- Tripled seasonal sales to $X.
- While continuing to serve as X, also managed A, B, and C.
- Wrote detailed specs and jargon-free *User Guide* for L.

Verbs/Action Words

Begin every action statement of every blurb with an action word. See Figure 5. Shop here for the most accurate and powerful action words to briefly describe your achievements. Choose your action words with care. *(text continues on page 45)*

Figure 5. Verbs/action words.

Abolish	Alert	Articulate	Blanket
Absorb	Align	Ascend	Blend
Accelerate	Allay	Ask	Block
Accept	Allocate	Assemble	Bolster
Access	Allow	Assert	Book
Accomplish	Ally	Assess	Boost
Accredit	Alter	Assign	Borrow
Accrue	Amass	Assist	Brace
Achieve	Amaze	Assure	Braid
Acquaint	Amend	Attain	Breed
Acquire	Amplify	Attend	Bridge
Act	Analyze	Attract	Brief
Activate	Anchor	Audit	Bring
Adapt	Announce	Augment	Broadcast
Add	Answer	Authenticate	Broaden
Address	Anticipate	Author	Budget
Adhere	Appeal	Authorize	Build
Adjust	Appear	Automate	Buoy
Administer	Apply	Avert	Buy
Admit	Appoint	Award	Calculate
Adopt	Appraise	Bake	Calibrate
Advance	Apprehend	Balance	Call
Advertise	Apprise	Barter	Calm
Advise	Approach	Bathe	Campaign
Advocate	Appropriate	Beat	Cancel
Affirm	Approve	Begin	Canvass
Affix	Arbitrate	Best	Capitalize
Aid	Arouse	Bid	Capture
Aim	Arrange	Bill	Care
Air	Arrest	Bind	Carry

Carve	Co-author	Confront	Cultivate
Cash	Cobble	Connect	Curb
Cast	Co-chair	Conserve	Cure
Catalog	Co-create	Consider	Curtail
Catapult	Code	Console	Customize
Catch	Collaborate	Consolidate	Cut
Categorize	Collate	Construct	Dazzle
Cater	Collect	Consult	Debate
Cause	Combine	Consummate	Debit
Caution	Comfort	Contact	Debug
Cede	Commemorate	Contain	Decentralize
Celebrate	Commend	Contest	Decide
Cement	Commission	Continue	Decipher
Centralize	Commit	Contract	Declare
Certify	Communicate	Contrast	Decline
Chair	Compare	Contribute	Decode
Champion	Compensate	Control	Decorate
Change	Compete	Convene	Dedicate
Channel	Compile	Convert	Deduce
Chart	Complement	Convey	Deepen
Charter	Complete	Convince	De-escalate
Check	Comply	Cook	Defend
Choose	Compose	Cooperate	Defer
Choreograph	Compound	Coordinate	Define
Chronicle	Compress	Copy	Deflect
Circulate	Compute	Copyedit	Defuse
Circumvent	Computerize	Correct	Delegate
Cite	Conceive	Correlate	Delight
Claim	Concentrate	Correspond	Delineate
Clarify	Conceptualize	Counsel	Deliver
Classify	Conclude	Count	Demonstrate
Clean	Condense	Cover	Demystify
Clear	Conduct	Craft	Depict
Climb	Confer	Create	Deploy
Clip	Configure	Credit	Depose
Close	Confine	Criticize	Deposit
Clothe	Confirm	Critique	Depreciate
Coach	Conform	Cull	Deprive

(continues)

Figure 5. *(continued).*

Derive	Dispute	Embrace	Estimate
Describe	Dissolve	Emerge	Evaluate
Design	Dissuade	Empathize	Evoke
Designate	Distinguish	Emphasize	Examine
Detach	Distribute	Employ	Excavate
Detail	Diversify	Enable	Exceed
Detain	Divert	Enact	Excel
Detect	Divest	Encounter	Exchange
Deter	Divide	Encourage	Excise
Determine	Document	End	Excite
Develop	Dominate	Endorse	Execute
Devise	Donate	Endow	Exercise
Devote	Double	Energize	Exert
Diagnose	Draft	Enforce	Exhibit
Diagram	Dramatize	Engage	Expand
Differentiate	Draw	Engender	Expedite
Direct	Dress	Engineer	Experiment
Disband	Drill	Enhance	Explain
Disburse	Drive	Enlarge	Explode
[funds]	Dry	Enlist	Exploit
Discern	Duplicate	Enliven	Explore
Discharge	Earn	Enrich	Export
Discipline	Ease	Enroll	Expose
Disclose	Eclipse	Ensure	Express
Discontinue	Edge	Enter	Expunge
Discover	Edit	Entertain	Extend
Discuss	Educate	Entice	Extract
Dismantle	Effect	Enumerate	Extrapolate
Dismiss	Elaborate	Equate	Extricate
Dispatch	Elect	Equip	Fabricate
Dispense	Electrify	Eradicate	Facilitate
Disperse	Elevate	Erase	Factor
[crowds]	Elicit	Erect	Familiarize
Display	Eliminate	Escalate	Fashion
Dispose	Elude	Escort	Feature
Disprove	Embed	Establish	Feed

Field	Grade	Improvise	Invigorate
File	Graduate	Inaugurate	Invite
Fill	Grant	Incite	Invoice
Finagle	Graph	Include	Involve
Finalize	Greet	Incorporate	Iron
Finance	Groom	Increase	Isolate
Find	Grow	Index	Issue
Finish	Guard	Indict	Itemize
Fit	Guide	Individualize	Join
Fix	Halt	Induce	Journalize
Focus	Halve	Infer	Judge
Fold	Hammer	Influence	Justify
Follow	Handle	Inform	Kindle
Forecast	Harness	Infuse	Knit
Forewarn	Hasten	Initiate	Label
Forge	Hear	Innovate	Land
Forgive	Heighten	Inoculate	Landscape
Form	Help	Inspect	Laud
Formalize	Highlight	Inspire	Launch
Formulate	Hire	Install	Launder
Forward	Hoist	Instill	Lead
Foster	Hold	Institute	Learn
Found	Hone	Instruct	Lecture
Frame	Honor	Insure	Legitimize
Freeze	Host	Integrate	Lend
Fulfill	House	Intensify	Lessen
Fund	Hypothesize	Intercede	Let
Furnish	Identify	Intercept	License
Further	Ignite	Interest	Lift
Gain	Illuminate	Interpret	Lighten
Garner	Illustrate	Interrogate	Limit
Gather	Imagine	Intervene	Link
Gauge	Impart	Interview	Liquidate
Generate	Impel	Introduce	Listen
Ghostwrite	Implement	Invent	Litigate
Give	Import	Inventory	Load
Glean	Impress	Invest	Lobby
Govern	Improve	Investigate	Locate

(continues)

Figure 5. *(continued).*

Log	Name	Overcome	Plant
Magnify	Narrate	Overhaul	Play
Mail	Navigate	Overturn	Plead
Maintain	Negotiate	Pack	Pledge
Make	Net	Package	Plow
Manage	Neutralize	Paint	Poll
Maneuver	Nominate	Pair [couple]	Portray
Manufacture	Normalize	Pamper	Pose
Map	Notarize	Paraphrase	Position
March	Note	Pare [cut]	Post
Mark	Notify	Part	Practice
Market	Nudge	Participate in	Praise
Master	Number	Partner with	Predict
Match	Nurture	Pass	Prepare
Maximize	Observe	Patch	Prescribe
Measure	Obtain	Patrol	Present
Mediate	Offer	Pattern	Preserve
Meet	Officiate	Pause	Preside
Mend	Offset	Pay	Presort
Mentor	Open	Peg	Press
Merge	Operate	Penalize	Prevail
Mind	Optimize	Penetrate	Prevent
Minimize	Orchestrate	Perceive	Print
Mix	Order	Perform	Prioritize
Mobilize	Organize	Permit	Probe
Model	Orient	Persevere	Process
Moderate	Originate	Persuade	Proclaim
Modernize	Outbid	Phase	Proctor
Modify	Outdistance	Photograph	Procure
Mold	Outdo	Pick up	Produce
Monitor	Outmaneuver	Pilot	Profile
Motivate	Outpace	Pinpoint	Program
Mount	Outperform	Pioneer	Progress
Move	Outrun	Pitch	Project
Mow	Outsell	Place	Promise
Multiply	Outsource	Plan	Promote

Prompt	Reassure	Relate	Return
Proofread	Rebuild	Relocate	Revamp
Propel	Rebut	Remand	Reveal
Propose	Recall	Remedy	Reverse
Prorate	Recast	Remit	Review
Prosecute	Receive	Remodel	Revise
Prospect	Recite	Remove	Revitalize
Protect	Reclaim	Render	Revive
Protest	Recognize	Renegotiate	Revolutionize
Prove	Recommend	Renew	Reward
Provide	Reconcile	Renovate	Rewrite
Provoke	Reconfigure	Reorganize	Risk
Prune	Record	Repair	Rivet
Pry	Recover	Replace	Rotate
Publicize	Recruit	Replicate	Rouse
Publish	Redeploy	Reply	Route
Pull	Redesign	Report	Run
Pump	Reduce	Reposition	Safeguard
Purchase	Reengage	Represent	Salvage
Pursue	Reengineer	Reprimand	Sanitize
Push	Refer	Reproduce	Save
Quadruple	Reference	Request	Scan
Qualify	Refine	Require	Schedule
Quantify	Refocus	Rescind	Schlep
Query	Reform	Rescue	Schmooze
Question	Reformat	Research	Scoop
Quicken	Refresh	Reserve	Score
Quiz	Refund	Reshape	Scour
Quote	Refute	Resist	Scout
Raise	Regain	Resolve	Screen
Rally	Regale	Respond	Script
Rank	Register	Restore	Scrutinize
Rate	Regulate	Restrict	Seal
Reach	Rehabilitate	Restructure	Search
React	Rehearse	Retain	Secure
Read	Reinstate	Retool	See
Realize	Reinvigorate	Retrain	Segment
Reap	Reject	Retrieve	Seize

(continues)

Figure 5. *(continued).*

Select	Solder	Sum	Trace
Sell	Solicit	Summarize	Track
Send	Solidify	Summon	Trade
Separate	Solve	Supersede	Train
Sequence	Soothe	Supervise	Transact
Serve	Sort	Supplement	Transcend
Service	Source	Supply	Transcribe
Set	Spark	Support	Transfer
Settle	Speak	Surpass	Transform
Sever	Specialize	Survey	Transition
Sew	Specify	Suspend	Translate
Shape	Spin	Sustain	Transmit
Share	Split	Sway	Transport
Sharpen	Sponsor	Sweep	Travel
Shatter	Spot	Switch	Treat
Shed	Spotlight	Synthesize	Trigger
Shelter	Spread	Systematize	Trim
Shelve	Spur	Tabulate	Triple
Shift	Stabilize	Tailor	Troubleshoot
Ship	Staff	Talk	Turn
Shlep	Stage	Tally	Turn around
Shmooze	Standardize	Tap	Tutor
Shop	Start	Target	Type
Shorten	State	Teach	Uncover
Shovel	Steer	Tell	Underscore
Show	Stem	Temper	Unearth
Showcase	Stimulate	Tend	Unify
Shrink	Stock	Terminate	Unite
Shut	Stop	Test	Unlock
Shuttle	Streamline	Testify	Unpack
Sign	Strengthen	Thank	Unravel
Simplify	Stretch	Theorize	Unveil
Sketch	Strip	Thrive	Update
Slash	Structure	Tighten	Upend
Slaughter	Study	Time	Upgrade
Smooth	Submit	Top	Uphold
Soften	Succeed	Total	Upholster

Up-sell	Vest	Warn	Wind
Urge	Veto	Wash	Wipe
Use	Vie	Watch	Wire
Usher	View	Water	Withdraw
Vacate	Vindicate	Weather	Withhold
Validate	Visit	Weave	Withstand
Vary	Voice	Weigh	Wow
Vault	Void	Welcome	Wrest
Veer	Volunteer	Weld	Wring
Vend	Vote	Widen	Write
Verify	Vow	Win	Yield

Volunteer Experience Section

Often overlooked or dismissed by candidates, volunteer experience is valuable information to a prospective employer if the skills used as a volunteer are relevant to an employer's requirements. For example, your volunteer work as a youth hockey coach is worth mentioning if you seek a paid teaching or coaching position, or any position requiring team-building skills. If a hiring manager reads of your service as a literacy tutor, he or she can easily infer your patience, a valuable skill. Likewise, if a reader sees you participated in an AIDS charity bike ride from Boston to New York City, he or she can glean from this your endurance and determination, valued skills in any organization.

Education Section

If you have completed one or more degrees, then include your graduation dates. Many employers interpret the absence of dates to mean (1) the candidate is attempting to hide his or her age and (2) the candidate is acknowledging that his or her age is something to be hidden. Why send these messages? Many talented, full-blown adults graduated from college before last Thursday. If you graduated in 1962, write it. Do you think the reader won't do the math some other way or won't figure it out when you meet? Don't hide your academic history. Write it proudly.

Employers hiring recent graduates from MBA, JD, and some other programs usually require each candidate to include his or her grade point average (GPA) on a résumé. Even if you are not a recent graduate, if you completed college or graduate school with a stellar GPA, you may choose to include it on your résumé. If you received honors, you may choose to include this, too. If you attended school at night for four years, this says a lot about you, so there is no reason to keep it a secret, either:

Education
6/87–5/91   Clark University, Metropolis, MA (nights)
                 Bachelor of Science, Economics, GPA 3.59
[Strike the TAB key after the end date on the first line and at beginning of the second line.]

If still in school, write "degree expected [month/year]" after the name of the degree:

Education
9/05–present   Clark University, Metropolis, MA
                 Bachelor of Arts, Music, degree expected 5/09
[Strike the TAB key after *present* on the first line and at beginning of the second line.]

If your résumé includes mention of a college degree (or "degree expected"), high school graduation is implied and thus need not be included.

If you have no college degree but some training, create a Relevant Coursework or Relevant Education/Training section (instead of an Education section) to include any relevant courses, seminars, or workshops you have completed, with the starting month and year (and ending month and year, if different) for each.

If you have no college education or relevant training but graduated from high school or earned your General Educational Development (GED), list it in your Education section. If you graduated from a specialized competitive-entry high school (for young artists or scientists, for example), specify this.

If you have no material for an Education section, focus on writing the other sections where your self-taught skills will shine through (work experience, volunteer experience, software skills, language skills, and so forth) and increase your knowledge and marketable skills by taking useful courses at a school near you.*

Inventions, Published Works, Seminars Section

If you have invented, published, or lectured, and if these accomplishments relate to your current career path, then include a section to briefly list them:

Published Works, Seminars

9/01	"Make Your Skills Jump off the Page" (seminar given at Metropolis University, Metropolis, NY)
11/00	"Résumés: Writing a Knock'em Dead Résumé" (article for ivillage.com)
1/00	"13 Truths about Résumés and Cover Letters" (article for click4careercoaching.com)

Software Skills Section

If you are not an information technology (IT) candidate, but you do use a personal computer (PC), then include on your résumé the operating systems (e.g., MS-DOS, Windows, MAC-OS), office applications (e.g., Word, Excel, Access, PowerPoint, Publisher, Netscape), and programming languages (e.g., C++, Java, Visual Basic, HTML, COBOL)

---

*An increasing number of schools and colleges now offer classes scheduled around the needs of working adults. Contact each school's financial aid office to learn how to get help with tuition, fees, books, child care, and other expenses while you attend.

you use. Omit version numbers; if you use one version, then you can learn another. Here is a sample:

Software Skills
MS-DOS, Windows, MAC-OS, Word, Excel, PowerPoint, Publisher, FrontPage, Explorer

(This Software Skills section implies the ability to *use/navigate* Windows.)

Some candidates will include a long list of software skills on their résumé, then send their cover letter and résumé in a handwritten envelope. Learn to print an envelope. It will make your software claims a lot more credible.

The point of this section is not to list every application you have ever used. It is simply to convey two facts: (1) you do not fear technology and (2) faced with any new software, all you need is a user guide and a little time to master it.

If the speed and accuracy of your typing are impressive and the position you seek demands these skills, then take the test at *www.typingtest.com* (free at the time of this writing) and include the error-free result (e.g., "Word (80wpm)") in this section.

If you are an IT candidate, you may naturally have a longer list of skills in this section. Use Software/Systems Skills (instead of Software Skills) as a heading, with subsections as needed:

Software/Systems Skills
Languages/Environments: PowerBuilder, Korn Shell, C, COBOL, Oracle SQLPlus, PL/SQL, Visual Basic, Visual InterDev (VB Script), CA-Librarian, CICS, TSO/ISPF, Focus, PL/1, MarkIV
Operating Systems: Unix AIX, MVS, DOS, Windows NT
Databases: Oracle, Access, ADR DataCom
Desktop Applications: Word, Excel, Netscape, Explorer
Machines: IBM 370/158, IBM 3033, IBM 3083/Model B CPU, PCs

(This Software/Systems Skills section implies the ability to *program* for Windows.)

Language Skills Section

If you are fluent in any language other than English, include a Language Skills section on your résumé. Specify whether you read, write, and/or speak the language. For example:

> **Language Skills**
> Spanish (read), French (read, write, and speak), German (speak)

If you have mastered American Sign Language or Braille, include it in this section, too.

Memberships Section

If your membership in an organization helps you build skills relevant to an employer, then include it.

If a membership (or volunteer experience) helps you effectively showcase marketable skills, then don't necessarily exclude it for fear of exposing other information. If, for example, you're actively involved in a group whose name reveals you may be lesbian, gay, bisexual, transgender, of a particular faith, or possess any other characteristic unrelated to merit—and if your role involves skills useful to an employer—write it proudly. Being ruled out for a job on the basis of any criterion other than merit is a useful warning. You wouldn't want to work for such employers anyway. It's their loss. Many hiring managers with a brain and a pulse will happily scoop up qualified people to help them compete in the marketplace.

What do you do for the organization? Briefly mention it:

> **Memberships**
> 9/01–present   Gay and Straight Alliance of Xtown, Xtown, NY
> Co-facilitate 6 meetings (2 groups, 3 sessions each)/month.
> Contribute Web content.

When deciding to include or exclude, the test is this: Is the information needed to make an effective pitch? If, in this case, you have already included on your résumé plenty of other examples of group facilitation skills and Web writing experience, you may choose to omit this membership. Similarly, if you only attend groups (vs. co-facilitate them) and visit the Web site (vs. contribute content to it), then, again: Is the information needed to make an effective pitch?

In each case, use your judgment to assess the risks and benefits of inclusion. Do not prejudge all prospective employers as racist, homophobic, anti-faith, and so forth.

References Statement?

Exclude "References available on request." Employers know this already.

Personal Information Section?

In the United States, listing one's age, height, and weight,* hobbies, interests, health, and marital or parental status on a résumé is generally a waste of the reader's time, and may be seen—depending on the organization's culture—as inappropriate, irrelevant, silly, and of absolutely zero interest to the reader. Your résumé is not an autobiography.

Rather than omitting all hobbies and interests, however, you may decide there are exceptions. Use your judgment. If a particular hobby or interest genuinely contributes to your relevant skills, include it. If you choose to include a Relevant Hobbies/Interests section, proceed with caution.

Artwork, Photos, Decorative Borders, and Line Art

Artwork and photos are not part of a résumé. If they are required by an employer, include them in a separate portfolio.

---

*Unless one seeks an acting, modeling, physical education, or law enforcement job.

Decorative borders and line art are similarly inappropriate on a résumé. Fair or not, to many readers there is a fine line between artistic/whimsical (sometimes suitable) and flaky/inappropriate (at no time suitable). Skilled graphic artists know that context is important. A résumé is not the proper context for decorative borders and line art.

Here are four sample résumés using some of the previously mentioned résumé sections. Remember: the sequence, number, and nature of the sections you include on your résumé will be based not on any samples but solely on your unique story.

Kyla Sample
123 Main Street, Metropolis, NY 10001-0001
phone: 123-456-7890, fax: 234-567-8901, e-mail: kylasample@domainname.com

Work Experience

10/05-present   Big Giant Company, Metropolis, NY
                       Director of Purchasing
Initiate sweeping vendor review and cut materials costs more than $4.2M/year.
Collaborate with sales, production, receiving, and suppliers to implement
just-in-time deliveries and eliminate $800K/year in carrying costs. Renegotiate
contracts and replace vendors to cut facility, travel, technology, and supply
costs $1.6M/year.

4/02-9/05   XYZ International, Metropolis, NY
                       Purchasing Manager
Launched, taught, and enforced purchase requisition system for use at all
levels to eliminate non-approved spending. Designed purchase order forms
to meet complex federal and international regulations. Developed secondary
suppliers for 100+ key materials to avoid sole sourcing. Managed 8 staff.
Served as Acting Director as needed.

7/96-2/02   ABC Inc., Metropolis, NY
5/99-2/02   Senior Buyer
7/96-4/99   Buyer

6/94-6/96   Little Tiny Company, Metropolis, NY
                      Assistant Buyer

Volunteer Experience

3/03-present   Tutor, Literacy Volunteers of America, Metropolis, NY

Education

9/97-5/99   Metropolis Business School, Metropolis, NY (nights)
                      Master of Business Administration

9/90-5/94   Metropolis University, Metropolis, NY
                      Bachelor of Science, Economics, *summa cum laude*

Memberships

9/02-present   APICS, The Association for Operations Management
8/02-present   NAPM, Institute for Supply Management

Software Skills

Windows, MAC-OS, Word, Excel, PowerPoint, Publisher, Netscape, Explorer

Language Skills

Read, write, and speak Spanish

Jason Case
123 Main Street, Metropolis, NY 10001-0001
phone: 123-456-7890, fax: 234-567-8901, e-mail: jasoncase@domainname.com

Education

9/05-present	MNO University, Metropolis, NY (nights and Saturdays) Master of Social Work, degree expected 5/07
9/02-5/05	XYZ University, Metropolis, NY (nights) Bachelor of Arts, Psychology, *magna cum laude*
9/00-5/02	ABC Community College, Metropolis, NY (nights) Associate of Arts, Human Services

Experience

6/04-present   Metropolis Supported Housing, Metropolis, NY
                              Life Skills Counselor
Co-facilitate 5 weekly group therapy sessions. Contribute to 120+ treatment plans. Help public assistance recipients, ex-offenders, and persons in substance abuse recovery improve communications skills, manage anger, prevent conflict, and move to self-sufficiency. Advocate for clients to get transitional benefits as they move to paid work.

12/02-5/04   Metropolis State Hospital, Metropolis, NY
                              Mental Health Aide
Helped 40+ clients with schizophrenia develop communications and time management skills, hygiene, sound diet, and medication compliance. Provided emotional support. Recorded observations for use by clinicians. Supervised group recreational activities.

7/00-6/02   Metropolis Cares, Metropolis, NY
                              Community Outreach Worker
Created and delivered presentations to 100+ schools, hospitals, and social service agencies. Grew client referrals 70% in 1 year. Co-developed pitches to prospective donors. Recognized for contribution to obtaining more than $1.6M in new donations.

Memberships

5/04-present   American Counseling Association
5/01-present   American Mental Health Counseling Association

Software Skills

Windows, Word, PowerPoint, Publisher, Netscape, Explorer

Terri Example
123 Main Street, Metropolis, NY 10001-0001
phone: 123-456-7890, fax: 234-567-8901, e-mail: terriexample@domainname.com

Goal
Transition to and establish career in technical sales.

Work Experience

9/03-present   WidgetLand, Metropolis, NY
                      Assistant Network Administrator
Help maintain server, Internet/e-mail, and software to support 120-user local
area network comprised of human resources, sales/marketing, customer
service, purchasing, accounting, and receiving/shipping applications. Train
staff on sharing data among disciplines to improve performance in all areas.
Initiate disaster plan to protect vital data.

12/02-present   Metropolis Technical College, Metropolis, NY
                      Technology Aide (part-time)
Support 600+ users of various skill levels on 40 PCs, 2 printers, 1 scanner,
1 fax, and 2 copiers. Help non-traditional students overcome fears of
computing. Troubleshoot tech issues. Inventory supplies to prevent shortages.
Select and install security software. Create popular "cheat sheets" for users to
more easily navigate common applications.

Volunteer Experience

1997   Girl Scouts of America, Metropolis, NY
                      Recognized for achieving highest cookie sales in
                      Metropolis.

Education

9/02-5/04   Metropolis Technical College, Metropolis, NY
                      Associate of Science, Computer Science

Continuing Education

3/05   Dale Carnegie Training, Metropolis, NY
                      How to Cold Call and Build New Customers

Memberships

1/04-present   Toastmasters International
12/02-present   Association for Computing Machinery

Software/Systems Skills

Windows NT, Novell, Word, Visual Basic, Access, HTML, Netscape, Explorer

Miles Instance

123 Main Street, Metropolis, NY 10001-0001

phone: 123-456-7890, fax: 234-567-8901, e-mail: milesinstance@domainname.com

Experience

9/04-present — MegaLoMart, Metropolis, NY
Customer Service Representative and
Front-End Supervisor
Manage cashiers, cash office, bridal registry, monogramming, and gift wrap services. Investigate and resolve customer inquiries on merchandise or service. Help hire and train 30+ staff. Awarded for managing highest volume sales ever during a single shift.

9/02-present — Shop and Get Out, Inc., Metropolis, NY (part-time)
Salesperson and Cashier, Accessories Department

6/01-8/01 and — Teeny Tiny Mart, Metropolis, NY
6/02-8/02 — Cashier and Stock Clerk

Education

9/04-present — Metropolis Business College, Metropolis, NY (nights)
Bachelor of Science, Business, degree expected 5/08

Software Skills

Windows, Word, Excel, Netscape, Explorer

Language Skills

Read, write, and speak Spanish

5

Deliver Your Message the Right Way to the Right Places

Whether, how, when, and where to send your résumé are decisions as important as the decisions you make as you design each element of its content.

Sending Your Résumé

Employers often receive résumés so unrelated to the requirements for an available position (and cover letters so devoid of enthusiasm) that they openly wonder why candidates even bothered to send them. This happens a lot.

Sending a résumé—no matter how well written—in response to an unsuitable opening is a common and easily preventable cause for receiving no invitation to interview. Ask yourself:

- Do I meet all or almost all requirements for the position?*
- Am I really interested in the work, hours, and location?

If either answer is no, then do not send your résumé. If both answers

---

*In a job ad, the words *preferred, helpful, desirable,* and *a plus* do not mean "required." Sometimes, candidates confuse these terms and, as a result miss out on many opportunities. Do not rule yourself out from responding to an ad because you don't have everything on an employer's wish list. Like everyone else, an employer may prefer lots of things. So what? Smart, caring, and enthusiastic candidates are easily trainable and often just what an employer needs. In the eyes of many hiring managers, these qualities easily outweigh the absence of one or two "preferred" items.

are yes, then respond to the ad or job listing by sending a Response Letter (see pp. 63–67) and your résumé to the employer.

Unless specifically prohibited, send your documents every way you can. This includes snail mail, fax, e-mail, and by hand. Repeated exposure shows perseverance and genuine interest.

Rather than sending your documents by all four methods at the same time, however, you may choose instead to wait a few days or even a week between methods to see in each case if fewer methods will generate a response. (When you can, avoid snail mail as the first in your sequence, though, since it is the slowest of the four.*) There's a fine line between perseverance and pestering; aim not to cross it.

Employers often receive e-mail attachments in file formats they cannot open. Such formats imply inconsiderate candidates. Do not assume employers have the time or the inclination to "unzip" or otherwise convert your files. E-mail your résumé either as a Microsoft Word attachment** or in the body of an e-mail message. Doing so implies a considerate candidate.

If you send an attachment, first name the file in a way that is helpful to the recipient. A file named "myresume" may be useful to you at home but is of little use to an employer receiving thousands of résumés. Instead, use an easily understandable naming protocol (e.g., "resumelastfirstmiddlename"). Doing so is a big help to the people receiving your information.

Although Microsoft Word attachments are now generally accepted when sending e-mail, some employers require you instead to send your résumé in the body of an e-mail message. Here's how to do it:

---

*When you do send snail mail, avoid using a postage meter. Using a meter may send two negative messages: (1) rather than having been thoughtfully selected, the recipient is merely one of many in a mass mailing and (2) you may inappropriately be using your current employer's postage meter, time, and other resources to find new work.

**Attaching your résumé to an e-mail message is a breeze. Using any e-mail program, click on COMPOSE or similar word and then look around for the word ATTACH. Usually to the right of ATTACH, you will see a button marked BROWSE. Click on BROWSE, go to MY DOCUMENTS, double-click on your résumé, then—if your e-mail program requires it—click on OK or ATTACH.

How to Send Your Résumé in the Body of an E-Mail

1. Using "Save As" in Microsoft Word, create a second version of your résumé in "text only" instead of "Word Document" format.

2. Remove italics, bold, and symbols, if any.

3. Delete tabs between text and replace them with one comma and one space.

4. "Align left" all text with a maximum of sixty-five characters and spaces per line.

5. Block (SHIFT-⇩) all text, copy (CTRL-C) it, and then paste (CTRL-V) it into the body of your e-mail.

6. Adjust it as needed in your e-mail.

7. E-mail it to yourself first. (Many candidates forget to do this.)

8. See how it looks on the screen when you receive it, and print it to see how it looks on paper.

9. Adjust it again as needed.

10. When your document looks great on screen and on paper, then block, copy, paste into a new e-mail, and send it to a prospective employer.

(Responding to job listings is not always the most effective way to find great work. See pp. 67-68 to learn about the often-forgotten Inquiry Letter.)

Whether responding or inquiring, call—and check the Web site, if there is one—to obtain the correct spellings for the current names and titles of the human resources manager and the relevant department manager, even for names you are convinced have only one possible spelling.

Job/Career Fairs and Reverse Job/Career Fairs

You may want to use your résumé at job/career fairs; proceed with caution when deciding whether to attend at all, however. The most successful such fairs (1) are free (beware if there is an admission fee),

(2) include a substantial number of employers, and (3) are sponsored by a reputable organization. If you are interested in working with non-profits, for example, then go to *www.idealist.org* and enter "career fairs" in the search box for a list of nonprofit career fairs.

Reverse job/career fairs, where candidates have booths and employers attend, are a recent phenomenon and these too are best when they (1) are free to candidates, (2) include many employers, and (3) are sponsored by a trusted organization.

Responding to Blind Ads

Some ads do not reveal an employer or headhunter name. Why? There are many reasons. Here are three: A small employer may be trying to save money on an ad by reducing the number of words the ad contains. Another (less innocuous) reason is that a less-than-reputable headhunter may be trawling for résumés for potential employer-clients. A third reason is that an employer may not want to reveal a strategically important opening to suppliers, competitors, clients, or prospects.

Whatever the reason, there are several ways to look for the missing information. Here are two: If an ad lists only a fax number, go to *www.google.com*. At *google.com*, (1) type the fax number (e.g., "123-456-7890" with the quotation marks) and get the result or (2) type "freeality reverse lookup" and use the free tools there to get the result. If you find the result is a headhunter, you may choose not to respond. (Here's why: Reputable headhunters tend to proudly advertise their identities rather than hide them using blind ads.) However, you may find in the results an employer name and phone number. If so, you can call for the correctly spelled name of both the human resources manager and the hiring manager. Your response letter will be one of only a few in the stack with this information.

If an ad reveals only an e-mail address as the contact, there are many ways to find out more. Here are two: Usually, the part of the address after @ is an active Web site address. Type it (the part after @)

into the "location" (Netscape) or "address" (Explorer) field in your Web browser, get the results, and learn more. If the portion of the address after @ is a community or mail site (e.g., *www.gmail.com, www.yahoo.com, www.hotmail.com*) rather than an employer Web site, then there's another way to learn more. Use *www.freeality.com* (or one of many other sites) to do a reverse lookup by e-mail address. Again, if you find the result is a headhunter, you may choose not to respond. However, you may find in the results an employer name and phone number. If so, you can call for the correctly spelled name of both the human resources manager and hiring manager. Again, your response letter will be one of only a few in the stack with this information.

If the ad contains only a post office box as contact, this is a giant red flag and you may not want to respond. Such ads may be from disreputable companies. However, if you decide to respond anyway, there is a way to learn more. Call the postal service in the city or town where the box is located. As of this writing, the postal service (in the United States) is required to disclose upon request the name of the owner of a post office box.

If the ad states only a newspaper's private box number as contact, this too may be a red flag. However, if you decide to respond anyway, there is little in this case you can do to discover the identity of the owner of the box unless you have a connection at the newspaper. Without asking anyone to break any rules, you can ask for the information, however, and a nice (or new) newspaper advertising department employee may provide it.

It is generally unwise to respond to requests for salary requirements (see pp. 71-72) or salary history (see pp. 72-75) when choosing to answer a blind ad. Giving such private data to an unnamed and unaccountable person or organization is an invitation to trouble.

If the job and the employer described in a blind ad strike you as familiar, if the ad reads like an upbeat version of your or a co-worker's present job, then it may help to recall the famous horror movie line, "The call is coming from inside the house." Think about it.

6

Cover Letters

You get only one chance to make a first impression. If you're like many candidates, you think it's when you walk into an interview, but it's really the moment a human resources or hiring manager glances at your cover letter. Few people will read even a perfect résumé if your cover letter has errors, is unclear, or is unfocused; and if in this case your résumé is left unread, there will be no in-person interview.

Cover Letters in General

In order to produce an error-free cover letter, be sure to remember these three items (excerpted here from page xvii as reminders):

1. Don't count on your spell-check. Spell-check is not an editor: *form* vs. *from* escapes spell-check, as does *their* vs. *there* vs. *they're*, among countless other such examples. If one mistakenly types *copletion* instead of *completion*, several versions of Microsoft Word will suggest replacing it with *copulation* instead of *completion*. Use a dictionary.

2. Don't skip the step of proofreading your finished product. In addition to rereading your documents from start to finish to check for clarity, also read them backwards to catch typos. This will slow your reading and allow you to focus on each word.

3. Don't overlook having other qualified people review your finished product. Have your documents reviewed by at least two other people (a) who routinely hire people as part of their work and (b) whose writing skills and candor you respect. Here's the hard part: listen to what they have to say. As writers, sometimes we have to delete cherished words and phrases to create the clearest, most focused documents. It often takes another qualified set of eyeballs to help with this.

Unless there is a specific prohibition on phone calls stated in an ad or listing, call for the hiring manager's current title and the correct spelling of his or her name. If the organization is big enough, there will be both a human resources name and title and a hiring department manager name and title (obviously the same person if you seek a human resources position)—get (and send to) both if you can. Ask to confirm the spelling even for names you think could have only one spelling. Chris could be Kris, Terry could be Terri, Mark could be Marc, John could be Jon, and Jason could be Jayson. Why not be seen as the one in 100 candidates who took the time to get it right?

Make it easy for the reader to recognize and reach you. Block (SHIFT-⇩) and copy (CTRL-C) your "heading" (name, address, phone, fax, and e-mail) from your résumé and paste (CTRL-V) it at the top of your cover letter. Sometimes, cover letters mistakenly get separated from résumés. If a cover letter is compelling enough, it may even generate a phone call without a résumé, but only if contact information is on the letter.

If you use a similar letter for more than one employer, remember to change the name and address in each letter. Candidates reveal lack of attention to detail by leaving a wrong name or address in what looks like—because it is—a carelessly assembled form letter.

Less is more. A long cover letter is often interpreted to mean, "The following résumé may not be too clear, so here are the important things from it I'd like you to know." Is this an admission you want to make? Instead, have a clear and focused résumé so your cover letter need not be a novel. Your cover letter needs only to capture and express your enthusiasm, getting the reader to look at your résumé. Do not restate chunks of your résumé in your cover letter.

Anyone who advises candidates to write a four-paragraph cover letter is probably not an employer. You are more likely to win the lottery than to have any employer actually read a four-paragraph cover letter. Less really is more.

Beware of using humor. Professional comedians are paid well for a reason: comedy is more difficult than it looks. Not only is comedy subjective (i.e., different people laugh at different things), but even one person will respond differently at different times to the same humor. Plus, there is the risk of unintentionally offending some readers. Overriding these issues, however, is the likelihood of appearing less than professional and, therefore, not being taken seriously as a candidate.

Have you ever written a sentence and then questioned yourself about its appropriateness? When this happens, it is a signal: your instincts are telling you something. Listen to them. If you question the appropriateness of something you have written, your reader may, too. Trust your instincts and remove or replace the sentence.

Express your enthusiasm. If you don't feel it, stop writing and ask yourself: Is this simply a bad time to write, or am I genuinely not enthused about this employer? If the former is the case, write at another time. If the latter is true, do not bother to write the letter at all. You will save yourself and the employer valuable time.

As you write:

- Express your enthusiasm without false praise.
- Express confidence without arrogance.

These nuances are at the heart of a winning cover letter.

By the way, sign your letter. Do not use a hokey font that purports to—and never does—look like handwriting. However, if you use PC fax software to send your letter directly from Microsoft Word to the employer, then there is no paper to sign. Instead, (1) specify "Via fax software to: [fax number]" under the recipient's address and (2) leave no blank lines between "Respectfully," and your typed name. Similarly, one cannot grab a pen and sign an e-mail message. You do not need to abandon the human touch completely, however. "Dear [Properly Spelled Contact Name]," and "Respectfully, [Your Name]" remain appropriate in e-mail messages to employers. Be one of the few who help prove that civility is not dead.

The following is a sample response letter text for you to play with and make your own. Copying it word for word will prove embarrassing for you if competing candidates use the same text. Your letter should reflect your personality.

Sample Response Letter

Jason D. Case
123 Main Street, Metropolis, NY 10001-0001
phone: 123-456-7890, fax: 234-567-8901, e-mail: xyz@domainname.com

[Date]

Properly Spelled Contact Name
Properly Spelled Current Title
Properly Spelled Employer Organization Name
Properly Spelled Street Address
Properly Spelled City, ST nine-digit Zip code

Re: Title of Advertised Position

Dear [Contact Name],

Given your requirements and my skills and experience, I may be the person you're after. I am enthusiastic about [Organization Name] and this work.

Would you be so kind as to please review my résumé and contact me soon? I eagerly await your reply. Thank you in advance.

Respectfully,

Jason D. Case

Do you think this is too brief? If so, I ask you to stop thinking like a candidate and start thinking like an employer. Imagine you are an employer. You are slogging through (not actually reading) hundreds of four-paragraph and even page-long response letters. Suddenly, you come across a breezy four-line letter. It stands out from the stack. It is visually different. It reflects a reader who respects your time. This candidate's résumé is worth a look.

The Unsung Hero of the Job Search: The Inquiry Letter

The inquiry letter is the unsung hero of the job search. It is arguably the least used and most powerful job search tool. Its use represents a very different way of looking for work. It changes the dynamic of the search, transitioning you to the role of an initiator from just one of many respondents.

New positions are frequently "in the pipeline"—being debated, created, and funded—well before a single job ad is placed. People are writing proposed job descriptions, fighting for budget dollars, and obtaining approvals for yet-to-be-advertised positions. A brief (!) enthusiastic inquiry letter and compelling résumé received during these planning stages often leads to a positive result for candidate and employer.

A well-written inquiry letter in a huge stack of response letters draws attention. Again, think like an employer: You're opening 100 response letters and one very different letter appears—it's oozing with enthusiasm, responding to nothing, from someone who just wants to be a part of your organization in whatever way you see fit—wouldn't that letter stand out from the stack? Of course, it would. It's always refreshing to see the initiative and genuine interest an inquiry letter represents.

Here is a sample inquiry letter text for you to play with and make your own. Copying it verbatim will prove embarrassing for you if competing candidates use the same text. Your letter should reflect your personality.

Sample Inquiry Letter

Kyla M. Sample
123 Main Street, Metropolis, NY 10001-0001
phone: 123-456-7890, fax: 234-567-8901, e-mail: xyz@domainname.com

[Date]

Properly Spelled Contact Name
Properly Spelled Current Title
Properly Spelled Employer Organization Name
Properly Spelled Street Address
Properly Spelled City, ST nine-digit Zip code

Dear [Contact Name],

Do you have or expect any open X positions in your organization that can make use of my skills and experience? I would like very much to be a part of [Organization Name]; I decided the best way to accomplish this is to ask you directly.

Would you be so kind as to please review my résumé and contact me soon? If you have no X positions available now or in the pipeline, but will point me toward other possibilities, I'd sure appreciate that, too. I eagerly await your reply. Thank you in advance.

Respectfully,

Kyla M. Sample

You may choose to include (briefly!) why you're interested. For example:

- I would like very much to be a part of X Hospital, the place that helped me deliver three of my children—now adults—into the world.

- A loyal subscriber for ten years, I would like very much to be a part of *X Magazine*.

Informational Interview Request Letter

Career path reconnaissance on the Web and at the library can yield much useful information, but even after you've read all you can about a line of work, you may still have some unanswered questions. It is often helpful to meet with an expert in your field of interest. An experienced perspective is invaluable.

Identify, ask, and meet with experts. Thorough career path reconnaissance can provide you with the names of experts in your field of interest. Send an informational interview request letter to several experts near you. There are many busy and well-paid experts kind and generous enough to give thirty minutes to help a newcomer.

Do not abuse this generosity by exceeding the allotted time or seeking a job from the expert. Instead, use the time to (1) ask thoughtful questions prepared in advance, (2) listen carefully to the answers, and (3) take notes. Your *only* goal at an informational interview is to gain insights into the field. An expert may also provide you with contacts in a position to help you secure a position, but this is certainly not required—so do not expect it. Plus, if you attempt mid-meeting to change the stated agenda and cajole job leads from the expert, you risk creating a powerful foe and developing a poor reputation in your new field of interest.

Learn all you can about the field before you meet the expert. Otherwise, you will be wasting his or her (and your) time on questions easily answered on the Web or at the library.

Prepare your questions before you send an informational interview request letter, because the letter may quickly yield an unexpected call from the expert offering to answer questions on the phone. Be ready.

Here is a sample informational interview request letter text for you to play with and make your own. Do not copy it verbatim. Again, your letter should reflect your personality.

Sample Informational Interview Request Letter

Miles J. Instance
123 Main Street, Metropolis, NY 10001-0001
phone: 123-456-7890, fax: 234-567-8901, e-mail: xyz@domainname.com

[Date]

Properly Spelled Contact Name
Properly Spelled Current Title
Properly Spelled Employer Organization Name
Properly Spelled Street Address
Properly Spelled City, ST nine-digit Zip code

Re: Request for an Informational Interview

Dear [Contact Name],

I seek to learn more about the possibility of transitioning to a career in X. I have read about this line of work in *The U.S. Occupational Outlook Handbook* and other places, but I realize there is no substitute for experience. My reconnaissance tells me you're an expert.

Would you be so kind as to meet with me for 30 minutes at a date and time convenient for you so I may ask you some prepared questions? I'd be very grateful. If your schedule does not permit this, would you refer me to a suitable colleague? Thank you in advance.

Respectfully,

Miles J. Instance

P.S. I enclose my résumé as an introduction and to give you a sense of my skills.

Error-free, clear, and focused cover letters are engaging, persuasive, powerful, and rare. You now have the information you need to craft yours.

7

The Final Three Pre-Interview Items: Salary Requirements, Salary History, References

Here's how you can prepare thoughtful responses to requests for salary requirements, salary history, and references—items for which on-the-fly answers will not suffice.

Request for Salary Requirements

Employers request salary requirements for several important reasons. Here are three:

1. They don't have time to interview people they can't afford to hire.

2. They don't want to waste the time of candidates they can't afford to hire. It's a small world: an applicant today may be a client tomorrow.

3. They want to see if the candidate can follow directions. This is the reason few people talk about. Employers want to see if a prospective employee will do as asked, rather than ignore a request simply because the task—in this case, writing a thoughtful answer—is challenging. This is why many employers discard response letters and résumés from people who fail to address this request.

Here's a sample response. Place your version at the end of your response letter.

> P.S. While I also place value on a number of other factors, I require a starting salary in the mid-$80s [or low $Xs, mid $Xs, high $Xs].

On the phone or in person, if asked about these "other factors," include: location, benefits, hours, working environment, company culture, opportunity for advancement, and any other noncash items of genuine importance to you. Although it's not required, you may also choose to include some of these items in parentheses after the word *factors* and before the comma in the sample given.

Notice that ranges are used, not specific numbers. This gives the hiring manager an opportunity to exercise his or her judgment and shows your flexibility as well.

Do not include a statement of salary requirements unless an employer first requests one. Doing so (1) is seen as inappropriate, (2) may remove you from consideration, (3) reveals too much information, and (4) may cost you money if the range for the position is above your stated requirements.

What if an employer reads my salary requirements and then ignores my résumé?

If this happens, then you are not a match for the current position, and your candor will have saved both you and the employer a lot of time and energy. Plus, many smart employers review and set aside rather than ignore the résumé of a skilled candidate they can't afford now; when a different position or more funding emerges, the candidate may be the perfect match.

Request for Salary History

Many candidates are annoyed by a request for salary history, and with good reason. Yes, it's intrusive. Yes, it's a red flag. Based on such a request, you may decide that the requesting organization is not the right employer for you. A request for salary history is the sign of an employer who mistakenly thinks there is some connection between previous and desired salaries. Such requests reflect a narrow view of the world and fail to recognize that (1) some people will gladly take a pay cut for the right position and (2) some people may have been significantly underpaid in the past and have no intention of continuing to be underpaid.

In any case, candidates risk having their response letters and résumés discarded by not responding to the request. Here is a sample salary history. Only provide a salary history if it is requested.

Scott A. Bennett
Confidential Salary History

Employer		Final Compensation
click4careercoaching.com, Metropolis, NY		
1/00–present	General Manager (part-time)	variable
XYZ Foundation, Metropolis, NY		
9/00–3/01	Career Developer	$45,000
ABC College School of Business, Metropolis, NY		
11/97–5/99	Career Services Counselor	$36,000
Self-employed, Metropolis, NY		
5/96–present	Freelance Writer and Lecturer	variable
FireSoft/Public Service Computer Software, Inc., Metropolis, MA		
8/94–4/96	President and Chief Operating Officer	$120,000
6/93–8/94	Sales and Marketing VP	$80,000
4/92–6/93	Sales Manager	$40,000
Tulip/Polymerics, Inc., Metropolis, MA and Cityville, MA		
10/90–4/92	Director of Purchasing	$67,000
Command Marketing/American Optical Corporation, Metropolis, CA		
4/89–7/90	Manager, Materials and Distribution	$42,000
1/87–4/89	Materials Project Manager	$35,000
1/86–1/87	Manager, Distribution, Western U.S.	$28,000
MetPath, Inc., Metropolis, CA and Eville, CA		
1/85–1/86	Operations Manager	$24,000
9/84–1/86	District Logistics Manager	$22,000
9/83–9/84	Logistics Manager	$18,000
6/83–9/83	Medical Courier	$12,000

Notice the absence of the starting month and year and ending month and year to the left of each employer's name. Unlike on a résumé, where such information is of use to the reader, it adds no value here and so can be excluded. Such dates to the left of each title are of use and important to include.

Elements of Compensation for Salary History

Use the final (not the starting) compensation number for each position. Compensation includes more than salary. Remember to include:

- Differentials for work locations or shift schedules
- Overtime pay (Many candidates forget to include this.)
- Monetary value of compensatory (comp) time
- Bonuses
- Commissions
- Stock options
- Employer contributions to retirement plan
- The annual monetary value of extraordinary benefits:
  - Portion of paid vacation above industry standard
  - 24/7 use of company car
  - Housing assistance
  - 100 percent tuition assistance
  - 100 percent health/disability/life insurance coverage with no paycheck deduction
  - Health club membership
  - Childcare services
  - Concierge services
  - Parking space in locations where parking is scarce (in several cities in the United States, this is worth from $2,400 to over $6,000 per year at the time of this writing)

Plus, if you declined to participate in an employer's health insurance plan because, for example, you were already covered under your spouse's/partner's plan, then the employer may have paid you a share of the resulting savings. If so, then these payments are part of your compensation, too.

References

A very popular reason employers request references is to see if a candidate is dumb enough to give bad ones. Few people talk about this, but now you know it. It's so easy to get this right, yet many candidates get it wrong.

Ask potential references before using them as references. Many candidates forget to do this, and people (even people who could've been excellent references) don't like such surprises. Prospective employers cannot always discern (nor should they have to) the difference between (1) the irritated voice of an unhappily surprised person and (2) a genuinely unenthusiastic reference.

Are you unsure how to ask someone to be a reference? If so, here are two ways:

1. "Are you willing to serve as a reference for me?"
2. "May I include your name and number when I provide references to employers?"

However you ask, after you ask, stop talking. Listen carefully to the response. Listen to both the content and the tone of the response. If a potential reference's response is anything other than genuinely enthusiastic, do not use him or her as a reference.

If he or she respects your work but performs poorly on the phone, proceed with caution. A prospective employer—or anyone else, for that matter—can easily confuse a naturally low-key or monotone voice with an absence of enthusiasm. Smart candidates prevent this confusion whenever possible. Follow your instincts. You may choose not to use the person as a reference, or to simply warn prospective employers. For example, "Please bear in mind when you call her that Georgette is quite soft-spoken, but she has consistently rated my work 'outstanding' on performance appraisals."

Here is a sample. Provide such data only if it is requested.

Scott A. Bennett
Professional References

John Lennon, VP, Operations (direct report)
XYZ Foundation, Metropolis, NY
123-456-7890 (office)

Paul McCartney, Director of Student Services (final direct report)
ABC College School of Business, Metropolis, NY
234-567-8901 (office)

George Harrison, Ph.D. (professor, professional ethics)
Professor, Counseling Psychology Program
Metropolis University/Downtown Campus, Metropolis, NY
345-678-9012 (office)

Ringo Starr, Ed.D. (professor, group counseling)
Adjunct Professor, Counseling Psychology Programs, Retired
Metropolis University/Uptown Campus, Metropolis, NY
456-789-0123 (home)

Limit references to persons for whom you have completed paid or academic assignments.

It's helpful to prospective employers to know with whom they are speaking: is it your manager ("direct report")? An instructor? After each name, explain the reference's relationship to you.

Be sure you are using the current phone number and only the one specified (office, home, or cell) by each reference.

Candidates whose work experience is with a family business face a special challenge. Although such references may understandably be viewed as less credible, include a relative as a reference if you worked for an extended period for the person. Explain the situation to each prospective employer requiring references.

We've examined the ways you can market your skills and experiences to employers. Next, let's look at how you market to *yourself*.

8

Marketing to Yourself

Many career writers often use the term "market yourself." Words matter, though, so let's clarify. What they really mean is "market your skills and experience," not "market yourself."

Another popular phrase used by career writers discussing salary is "What are you worth?" Again, words have meaning, and clarity is excellence. These writers really mean "What are some employers paying for a specific set of skills and experience?"

Why are these distinctions important? Because inaccurate but commonly used phrases such as these feed into the crazy and widely held notion that "I am my work." If you believe you are your work, then what are you when you are out of work?

"I am my work" is just one example of the many crazy ideas we quietly tell ourselves again and again for years. What we tell ourselves—that is, how we market *to* ourselves—is at least as important as how we market our skills and experience to employers.

If you believe you can't find work, you are likely to construct a résumé and do other things that will help you reinforce your belief. Few people do things in opposition to their own beliefs.

Do you recognize any of this thinking?

- I am my work.
- Without my work I am nothing.

- I can't find work.
- I'm too young for any employer to hire me.
- I'm too old for any employer to hire me.
- I'm too old to start a new career.
- If I were a minority, I would get the job.
- If I were a white male, I would get the job.
- I'm underqualified.
- I'm overqualified.
- Most of the jobs out there are beneath me.
- Employers feel threatened by my skills and experience.
- Employers think former entrepreneurs can't work for others.
- I was fired, and I'll never find another job.
- I was laid off, and I'll never find another job.
- Employers don't understand the duties of a working parent.
- I've sent out lots of résumés and had no luck. See?
- It's political. It's who you know, not what you know.
- The longer it takes, the less likely I will ever find a job.
- There are no jobs out there for me.
- Each day I remain unemployed proves I can't find another job.
- My search efforts shouldn't have to be like a full-time job.
- I should have now the job and salary I want to have.
- Employers should respond to my résumé.
- If I do not get a response from Company X, it will be awful.
- An employer must call me this week.
- If I don't get a job this week, it will be awful. I can't stand it.

None of these beliefs really serves the believer. Think about your beliefs about yourself, others, and the world. How are these beliefs working out for you?

How we react to and handle events is determined not by the events themselves but by how we view the events, often through the prism of our deeply held irrational beliefs. Although humans have a natural tendency to collect and nurture wacky beliefs, we also have the capacity to identify, examine, and replace those wacky beliefs with effective rational beliefs.

For more information, read *A Guide to Rational Living* by Albert Ellis and Robert Harper (North Hollywood, Calif.: Wilshire Book Company, 1998).

Conclusion: You're the Carpenter

This and other books, Web sites, videos, software, assessment instruments, even counselors and coaches are merely tools in a toolbox. You are the carpenter. The choices are yours. The process of examining and developing your skills, interests, and values and actively constructing a career in light of these is a process owned 100 percent by you. I encourage you to wear this book out and let the building begin.

Appendixes

More Examples of Effective Position Descriptions/Blurbs

View the following examples as food for thought, not material to be copied into your résumé. Notice the unique accomplishments of each candidate; because of this uniqueness, there exists no single blurb for every paralegal or every project manager or every coordinator or every nurse or every person in any position. Anyone who tells you otherwise (and gives you pages of boilerplate material to plop into your résumé) is underestimating your uniqueness. Employers can usually discern the difference between a thoughtlessly copied generic description and a genuine one resulting from careful thought. As the reader, you can infer a variety of skills from the following examples—although the blurbs contain no vague claims of skills (i.e., no hollow self-puffery, see pp. 22–26)—just concrete examples of skills in action.

If presented on an 8½ x 11-inch résumé page with 1-inch margins, most of the following examples (1) use no more than six lines of text, the most that's needed to convey the highlights of nearly any position and (2) contain no orphans (single words appearing on the last line of a blurb). As you craft your unique blurbs, keep them within six lines of copy and avoid orphans.

7/96–present   Company A, Metropolis, NY
                Director of Treasury Sales
Direct foreign exchange and money market product sales. Launch
global sales initiatives, using multi-site synergies to increase margins
by $6M. Successfully integrate 2 culturally disparate sales forces and
streamline processes, resulting in 200% margin increase and smaller
staff able to serve 57% more customers. Lead e-commerce
implementation project team. Collaborate with legal staff to design
and communicate changes needed to conform to complex and
changing accounting standards.

6/86–8/86   Hospital B, Metropolis, NY
               Occupational Therapy Aide
Built thriving occupational therapy program for unit of 32 long-term
patients with schizophrenia. Persuaded doubtful colleagues of
program value by generating rapid, observable positive results.

10/93–6/96   Company C, Metropolis, NY
               Vice President, Foreign Exchange Sales Manager
Re-engineered foreign exchange desk to handle added volume
without added staff. Managed trade shows and seminars. Co-led risk
management systems team to source and implement front- and
back-end systems and manage accounting and reconciliation issues.
Centralized order system to create a genuine 24-hour global
network, eliminating need for separate European night desk. Trained
100+ new dealers.

4/02–present   Non-profit D, Metropolis, NY
               Coordinator, Search and Placement, X Program
Help persons with physical and/or mental illnesses move themselves
from welfare to work. Institute "Active Seeker Agreement," statement
of requirements for candidates and staff. Streamline procedures to
eliminate excess paper, generate accurate data, and meet changing
city, state, and federal requirements. Establish phone/PC/resource
bank. Co-develop pre-employment curriculum. Manage
pre-employment trainer, job developers, retention staff, interns,
and volunteers. Serve as Acting Director in absence of director.

4/93–present   Company E, Metropolis, NY
                   Vice President, Operations
Apply planning to inventory control, import/export operations,
and HR. Integrate systems to provide instant tariff updates,
transaction reports, and cost analyses. Reduce headcount by 30% in
24 months. Manage relationships with manufacturing, fulfillment,
and distribution vendors. Implement protocols to meet food/drug,
agriculture, and customs requirements in 30 countries. Obtain
highest U.S. Customs compliance ratings. Direct website design to
give clients real-time delivery and account data.

2/88–8/94   Hospital F, Metropolis, NY
                   Occupational Therapist, XYZ Psychiatric Clinic
Provided treatment to all acute/homicidal/suicidal inpatients of
mixed age and diagnoses. Taught theories and roles of psychiatric
occupational therapy to rotating medical staff. Supervised 15
students. Facilitated Life Skills groups for long-term chronic
populations emphasizing stress management, time management,
social skills, motivation, leisure planning, and problem solving.
Coordinated multidisciplinary treatment.

10/00–present   Non-profit Agency G, Metropolis, NY
                   Director, XYZ Program
Turn around failing program to help persons with physical and/or
mental illnesses move themselves from welfare to work. Examine
operations, establish clear requirements, and train/replace staff
as needed to (1) prevent program closure and (2) efficiently
perform assessment, medical review, case management, education
(ABE/GED/ESL/PC Skills/Pre-employment), search and placement,
retention, and billing. Generate accurate data to meet changing city,
state, and federal requirements. Manage/develop 40 staff.

9/91–9/94   Mortgage Company H, Paris, France
                   Manager of European Transactions
Audited debtor firms to facilitate prevention of defaults and
bankruptcies. Examined operations of Swiss bank targeted for
purchase. Connected French entrepreneurs with suitable lenders.

8/89–9/91   Company I, Paris, France
                   Executive Vice-President and Managing Director
Managed the import, marketing, sale, and distribution of decorative
articles. Directed US$ 8M in sales, 4 offices, and 20 employees.

9/98–present   Medical Company J, Metropolis, NY
                   Senior Information Consultant
Provide all research. Establish Information Center procedures to
serve 6 sites. Maintain electronic filing system. Prepare and
implement recommendations on projects ranging from systems
migrations to storage requirements.

1/98–11/99   Food Company K, Metropolis, NY
                   Data Consultant, Business Information Services
Participated in development of Intranet catalog. Refined, updated,
and expanded classification scheme and corporate taxonomies.
Designed customized tools to create hierarchies and monitor
accuracy and consistency.

10/93–1/98   Medical Company L, Metropolis, NY
                   Information Consultant, Decision Support Services
Rapidly fulfilled complex information requests using print and
electronic resources. Gained expertise in organizational and
knowledge management activities.

6/94–8/95   Holding Company M, Metropolis, NY
                   Legal Assistant, Assistant to Corporate Secretary
Processed Securities and Exchange Commission filings. Summarized
depositions. Performed case cite checking. Maintained litigation files.
Recorded and tracked employee stock purchases.

8/00–present   Technology Company N, Metropolis, NY
                   Client Relationship Manager
Define and implement procedures to serve publishers, online
resellers, and end-users of applications software for Xs [electronic
devices]. Manage client service staff. Select and implement use
of salesforce.com to log calls. Source, extensively train, and
remotely supervise India call center vendor to meet 1 major
client's requirements.

8/92–6/94   Bank O, Metropolis, NY
                   Operations Specialist
Converted from temporary to permanent based on performance.
Processed mortgage applications. Performed credit checks. Created
database to track existing loan files.

2/79–8/89   Moving Company P, Rome, Italy and Paris, France
                   President
Provided moving services to French military. Managed $10M in sales,
3 offices, and 35 staff.

12/96–present   Company Q, Metropolis, NY and Paris, France
11/98–present   General Director, Metropolis, NY
Create first U.S. store for French retail fashion chain. Manage all real
estate, merchandising, staffing, marketing, and accounting. Achieve
sales of $500/square foot. Serve as liaison with Paris headquarters.
12/96–11/98   NY General Director, Paris, France
Obtained orientation and training in all business areas at corporate
headquarters.

6/87–5/88   Bank R, Metropolis, NY
                   Vice President, Chief Forward Dealer
Designed and implemented first online, real-time system to provide
position, profitability, and gap analyses for all foreign exchange
exposures. Strengthened communication between traders and IT staff
to test new applications. Managed strategic and foreign exchange
trading desks.

5/89–7/90   Bank S of England, Metropolis, NY
                   Senior Foreign Exchange Dealer
Managed cross-currency and strategic trading desks. Designed foreign
exchange training program. Trained 21 new dealers.

6/97–5/00   Retail Chain T, Metropolis, NY
                   Assistant Store Manager
Trained and managed 150. Supervised merchandising, customer
service, personnel, cash control, and internal and external loss
prevention. Monitored local competition and adjusted pricing and
presentation as needed. Audited 2 sites to ensure compliance with
laws, company standards, policies, and procedures.

3/93–12/95   Health Food Store U, Metropolis, NY
                  Community Outreach Coordinator
Created and delivered seminars and workshops on health and
nutrition awareness to educators, students, homemakers, and
community organizations. Collaborated with area non-profits (e.g.,
American Heart Association, YMCA) and hospitals (e.g., XYZ
Hospital) in support of their respective missions.

2/91–5/93   Company V, Hong Kong
                  Consultant
Conducted in-depth economic research to assess viability of client
investments. Helped clients negotiate complex licensing and
partnership agreements and plan investment projects.

7/93–4/99   Cable Company W,
                  Hong Kong and Johannesburg, South Africa
2/98–4/99   General Manager, Sales and Marketing,
                  Johannesburg, South Africa
Directed all business development, including planning and marketing
strategies. Managed introduction, pricing, promotion, and branding
of telecomm services. Defined, recommended, and managed upgrade
of customer service and billing system, in advance of deadline and
under budget. Favorably renegotiated terms with local venture
partners, forming Cable XYZ (South Africa) Ltd. Reported directly
to CEO.
2/95–2/98   Deputy Chief Representative,
                  Johannesburg, South Africa
Served as second-in-command of all business development. Built
solid political support, successfully petitioning government for
permission to rapidly establish offices. Developed alliances, partners,
and new business, helping establish firm nationally as recognized
industry leader. Negotiated US$ 207M venture project with dominant
state-owned carrier. Prospected and closed competitive US$ 1M
gateway access deal for client. Met stringent regulations of local and
national government agencies.

                                                      (continues)

7/93–1/95   Assistant Manager, Business Development,
                   Hong Kong
Formulated and implemented strategies to expand business to South
Africa. Identified, built, and expanded relationships with local
partners and corporate clients. Conducted successful presentations
and training programs, persuading local partners and national
government of benefits of foreign investment. Researched and
evaluated investment opportunities. Created business proposals with
demand and revenue forecasts. In 1 year, doubled client base for
international voice and data services.

4/89–8/93   X University, Metropolis, NY
                   Administrator, Graduate Recruitment
Introduced software to improve applicant-screening process. Trained
colleagues on use of office applications. Managed complex logistics
for high volume of candidates and screeners. Organized results of
PC-based Myers-Briggs personal style measure. Designed recruitment
literature and managed its production and distribution. Performed
outreach to universities and recruiters.

4/86–4/89   Company Y, Metropolis, NY
                   Administrator, Business Information Unit
Automated interlibrary loan system. Searched, retrieved, and maintained research for worldwide staff. Extracted relevant data from daily
newspapers to create timely organizational bulletins.

8/95–8/96   Retail Chain Z, Metropolis, NY
                   Front-end Manager
Managed cashiers, cash office, bridal registry, monogramming, and
gift wrapping services.

8/02–present   Non-profit A, Metropolis, NY
                   Instructor, ABE (Adult Basic Education) and
                   GED (General Educational Development)
Provide ABE and GED instruction to help persons with physical
and/or mental illnesses move themselves from welfare to work. Strive
to (1) set example by attendance, promptness, boundaries, and social
skills and (2) create a safe space, an environment of mutual respect,
and kindness conducive to active learning.

10/99–7/02   Non-profit B, Metropolis, NY
                Instructor, Job Readiness
Initiated and facilitated work-based education including job
readiness, life skills, ABE, and ESL (English as a Second Language)
for difficult-to-employ adults. Developed intra-agency work
experience sites for students. Trained, evaluated, and mentored
interns with barriers to competitive employment.

9/97–7/99   Non-profit C, Metropolis, NY
                Pre-employment Trainer, Supervisor of
                Employment Specialists
Managed four staff in service of moving persons with developmental
challenges into supported work settings. Initiated and crafted
curriculum for and facilitated pre-employment training. Edited
pitches to employers, including testimonials and tax credit data. Met
city, state, and federal reporting requirements.

5/97–10/00   Non-profit D, Metropolis, NY
                Consultant (part-time)
Analyzed 50 businesses owned/operated by consumers with mental
illnesses. Implemented changes to cut costs and raise revenues.
Established protocols for budgets and contract and grant
administration. Wrote approximately $300K in successful grant
proposals. Served as Acting Director of XYZ Housing (5/97–4/98), a
50-unit scattered site apartment program. Designed and supervised
vocational program for psychiatric and substance abusing tenants.
Conducted home visits including functional assessments, behavioral
contracting, and cognitive and vocational screenings. Managed 4 case
managers and 2 staff.

8/93–5/96   Petroleum Company E, London, England
                Administrator, Organization Effectiveness Unit
Appraised security and reception functions. Organized travel,
meetings, and worldwide conferences for 40 executives. Assembled,
produced, and monitored budget. Prepared and delivered
presentations. Supervised 6 staff.

8/95–12/96   Law Firm F, Metropolis, NY
                Legal Assistant
Prepared certificates of incorporation, merger and acquisition
documents.

5/86–present   Financial Services Company G, Metropolis, NY
7/98–present   Vice President, Administration &
                   Financial Reporting
Develop and support custom applications for Controllers to meet
complex weekly, monthly, year-end, and ad hoc management
reporting requirements. Provide clear easy-to-use menu-driven
interfaces. Standardize reporting to increase process efficiencies.
12/94–7/98   Assistant Vice President, Strategic Business
                 & Evaluation Group
Designed quarterly client revenue and product revenue tracking
systems. Collected data from internal and external sources to create
integrated decision-making tools for senior executives. Created
headcount reporting and analysis tool for Human Resources.
Produced Intranet content for CFO with detailed corporate
budget guidelines.
2/92–12/94   Associate, Distributed Financial Systems
Managed migration of budget system from mainframe to client/server
environment. Served as liaison among programmers and financial
analyst to develop reporting and maintenance utilities.
6/89–2/92   Technical Support
Thrived amid departmental transitions (serving both Distributed
Application/Technology Support and Corporate Budgeting), in
service of forecasts/budgets in client/server environment.
5/86–6/89   Systems Analyst, Corporate Budget
Trained and supported all levels of management on computing.
Created graphically advanced financial presentations. Participated in
migration to Windows operating system in LAN environment.
Evaluated and recommended suitable software applications and
hardware.

6/96–present   Manufacturing Company H, Metropolis, NY
10/99–present   Manager of Information Services and Webmaster
Lead team to provide Web-based solutions for multiple constituencies
and initiatives. Manage e-business strategic plans for Intranet sites.
Collaborate on content management, portals, and document
management. Chair 80-member group on data management and
business intelligence.
3/97–10/99   Information Specialist and Webmaster
Wrote *XYZ* for 500+ staff. Served as Editor of *Compliance Quarterly*.
Managed secretary, interns, and vendors. Produced content for,
maintained, and marketed 3 Web sites. Provided custom research for
senior staff in response to 1,200+ requests/year.

(continues)

6/96–3/97   Librarian
Initiated and developed Quality & Compliance Services Library in
service of worldwide quality and regulatory affairs staff. Managed
cataloging, acquisition/collection development and budget.

2/98–11/99   X Device Services Company I, London, England
                   General Manager and Manager, Technical Support
Managed 8. Introduced and enforced protocols for technical support,
human resources, finance, and advertising. Selected and adapted new
accounting application (Sage) to facilitate coherent reporting on all
aspects of transactions. Installed software (Office Talk) to more
efficiently manage e-mails and client service schedules. Designed and
maintained website. Designed ads and vigorously promoted firm's
services. Trained staff and clients in use of X brand devices.

12/96–4/99   Title Company J, Metropolis, NY
                   Project Manager
Managed 400+ UCC filings/week. Prepared files to meet complex
jurisdictional requirements. Coordinated searches. Met time-sensitive
requirements of attorneys and paralegals. Trained 8.

8/99–present   Computer Service Company K, Metropolis, NY
                   Owner and Computer Technician
Install, configure, upgrade, diagnose, troubleshoot, repair, and
perform preventive maintenance on PCs and associated operating
systems, applications software, printers, peripherals, and networks.
Serve as local subcontractor for manufacturer warranty work. Meet
and exceed numerous service standards. Maintain financial records.
Create ads and earn referrals to obtain direct clients.

9/92–present   Self-employed, Metropolis, NY
                   Guest Lecturer, Subject X (part-time)
Teach at New York University (NYU), Mercy College, Dominican
College, Long Island University (LIU), and State University of New
York (SUNY) Health Science Center at Brooklyn (a.k.a. Downstate
Medical Center).

9/81–6/85   Metropolis University, Metropolis, NY
                   Teaching Assistant, Biophysics (part-time)
Conducted advanced biophysics seminars for physicians/full
professors/doctoral candidates.

1/96–5/98   Metropolis Cable Network, Metropolis, NY
                   Account Executive
Generated $3M in new business. Tripled revenues from $500K to
$1.5M. Clients included BMW, UPS, Benetton, Kodak, and Sprint.

2/94–12/95   *Metropolis Magazine*, Metropolis, NY
                   Sales Representative
Developed and built up Home Furnishings, Entertainment, and
Atlantic City categories. Sold over 100 pages of advertising/year.

[Notice the choice here to emphasize customer service instead of merchandising.]

8/93–9/94   Retail Chain L, Metropolis, NY
10/93–9/94   Assistant Merchandise Manager
8/93–10/93   Customer Service Supervisor
Supervised schedules, front-end, store safe, petty cash, deposits,
and seasonal department. Managed up to 50 staff. Shared
Operations Manager duties, including recruiting, training, supplies,
and maintenance.

[Notice here that not every position requires a blurb.]

1/95–10/99   United States Army, Hospital M, Fort ABC, NY
3/98–10/99   Head Nurse, Family Practice Clinic
Managed high-volume operation with 400+ clients/week. Served as
liaison among patients, families, providers, and vendors.
2/96–2/98   Labor and Delivery Staff Nurse
Supervised 4. Conducted childbirth education classes. Participated in
new product studies.
1/95–1/96   Staff Nurse, Male Surgical Ward

[See several positions summarized here in one slightly longer-than-
usual blurb.]

4/85–11/98   Company N, Metropolis, NY
After providing engineering support, sales support, and direct client
care, managed 42 sales staff and established relationships with 75
external distribution firms. Routinely exceeded sales quotas.
Promoted synergies among sales and operations. Established
protocols to dramatically cut travel expenses. Developed and
conducted sales and technical training. Selected sites and managed
complex logistics for trade shows worldwide. Collaborated to create
marketing literature and programs. Initiated and executed strategic
plans in concert with subsidiaries.

4/93–11/98	Director of Sales, Technical Sales, and Sales Training Programs
3/91–4/93	Manager, International Sales
7/89–3/91	Sales Specialist, International
10/86–7/89	OEM Product Sales Support Specialist
4/85–10/86	Engineering Technician

[Here is another example describing multiple positions with one
blurb. The blurb also effectively positions the candidate's exit.]

| 4/87–present | Company O, Metropolis, NY |
| 4/98–present | Lead Advisor, W, X, Y, and Z |

Initiate and develop applications to accelerate communication among
human resources, payroll, and sales. Co-develop system to streamline
sales territory assignments and changes. Develop applications for
system security, contact management, account management, and direct
marketing data. Evaluate and select software tools. Provide technical
support to user support staff. Train users, programmers, and analysts
of various skill levels. Thrive amid 4 mergers/acquisitions. Decline
recent offer to join company's relocation to Iowa. Provide seamless
transition to successor (TBD, estimated 1/01).

4/91–4/98	Senior Advisor, X, Y, and Z
4/89–4/91	Systems Analyst, X and Y
4/87–4/89	Senior Programmer, X

[Here is another example using one blurb to describe multiple positions.]

2/90–present   Company P, Tokyo, Japan
Establish Singapore presence. Recruit 600+ engineers and supervisors
from 25+ countries for worldwide assignments. Manage evaluations,
reassignments, in-house sales incentives, and payroll. Negotiate
leases. Meet local tax and regulatory requirements. Implement
software and protocols to operate on time and under budget, earning
Corporate Presidential Award for achievements. Re-deployed to
evaluate, correct, and prevent critical materials delays; launch
Slovakia operations; and run procurement for Iran facility. Promoted
to run entire division.
9/98–present   Manager, Construction Division, Tokyo, Japan
10/97–9/98   Iran Refinery Procurement Coordinator,
                      Tokyo, Japan
6/97–9/97   Administration Manager, Bratislava, Slovakia
4/96–6/97   Buyer, Tokyo, Japan
11/95–4/96   Special Expeditor, Tokyo, Japan
4/95–11/95   Singapore Administration Manager, Tokyo, Japan
2/90–4/95   General Manager, Singapore

[Here is another example using one blurb to describe multiple positions.]

7/77–8/89   Company Q, Tokyo, Japan
Wrote and edited engineering standards for companywide use.
Applied standards knowledge to increasing role in materials
management, including inventory, document control, logistics, and
procurement for 4 locations. Directed US$ 70M budget. Sourced and
negotiated complex multinational subcontracts. Collaborated on
elaborate presentations to update clients and facilitate new projects.
Implemented new software to streamline operations, earning Award
for Excellence in Technology Application.
4/88–8/89   Manager, Marketing Materials, Tokyo, Japan
4/87–4/88   Controls Manager, Safwa, Saudi Arabia
5/85–4/87   Assistant Controls Manager, Tokyo, Japan
                     and Safwa, Saudi Arabia
5/83–5/85   Administration Supervisor, Tokyo, Japan
1/83–5/83   Project Control Staff, Tokyo, Japan
11/79–1/83   Assistant Controls Manager, Tokyo, Japan and
                     Safwa, Saudi Arabia
7/77–11/79   Writer and Editor, Standards and Manuals,
                     Tokyo, Japan

[Notice how lateral and downward position changes (in lieu of layoff) are handled here.]

> 1/79–3/89   Company R, Metropolis, NY
> Co-developed and implemented contracts administration staff training adopted for nationwide use. Conveyed training in print, by phone, and in person. Cut service response times by evaluating problems and swiftly deploying suitably skilled technicians to clients. Thrived amid complex organizational changes. Served in seven positions, ranging from Receptionist to Regional Contracts Administrator.

[Notice how an "additive promotion" with dual responsibilities is explained here.]

> 12/79–3/93   Company S, Metropolis, NY
> 1/88–3/93   Director of Operations
> While continuing to serve as Traffic Manager, also managed complex trades, hedging physical position against futures position to profitably negotiate coffee imports and sales to domestic manufacturers. Initiated creation of relational database to track transactions, including inventory, delivery, and invoicing.
> 12/79–1/88   Traffic Manager
> Directed coffee imports and national distribution network. Negotiated freight contracts with more than 30 trucking, rail, and ocean carriers. Managed relationships with 13 external warehouses across the country. Obtained approvals from U.S. Customs, U.S. FDA, and clientele with rigorous product standards.

[Notice how the "additive promotion" from supervisor to assistant director is handled.]

8/94–10/00   Hospital T, Metropolis, NY
10/98–10/00   Clinical Director,
                Occupational/Recreational/Arts Therapies
Planned and directed clinical services and managed budgets for 15 psychiatric and substance abuse programs. Initiated agreements with 25 schools to engage 100+ graduate/undergraduate occupational therapy students. Managed Continuous Quality Improvement for Psychiatry Department. Managed 23.
10/96–10/98   Assistant Director,
                Occupational/Recreational/Arts Therapies
Supervisor role extended to second facility (Hospital X).
8/94–9/96   Supervisor,
                Occupational/Recreational/Arts Therapies
Reorganized for more cost-effective and integrated services in drug/alcohol/women's detoxification inpatient and dual diagnosis outpatient programs. Initiated quality assurance measures. Supervised 8 therapists. Trained staff on managed care protocols. Managed caseload. Conducted in-service training. Authored—and trained staff to use—*ABCDE Workbook* for persons with mental illness and chemical addiction. Designed, conducted, presented, and published research. Served as Acting Director in absence of program director.

A Special Note to Homemakers

Whether you're male or female, returning to paid work or seeking paid work for the first time, you may think you don't have the skills needed to thrive in today's competitive job market.

Hmm . . . let's look at the facts. Homemakers have many skills to offer. Smart employers look beyond paid work to any evidence of transferable skills. Here is a giant sample position description/blurb (much larger than is appropriate for an actual résumé) containing many examples of action statements for homemakers. Each action statement gives the reader specific evidence of transferable skills. Use these examples as food for thought as you craft your own action statements unique to you.

On an 8½ x 11-inch résumé page with 1-inch margins, keep your position description/blurb to within six lines and avoid orphans (single words appearing on the last line of a blurb).

1/00–present   Homemaker, Metropolis, NY
Manage schedules and logistics for family of five. Balance priorities to create and implement budget. Motivate, coach, and counsel children. Teach and model ethics. Work with teachers to closely monitor academic performance of children. Plan, organize, and co-supervise extracurricular school activities. Mediate disputes among family members and facilitate solutions. Shop for clothing, food, and supplies. Prepare and serve nutritious meals for five. Coordinate medical
(continues)

care for all family members. Establish clear requirements and discipline children. Drive children to schools, team sports, music lessons, and more. Negotiate with suppliers. Pay invoices. Reconcile accounts. Arrange for home and vehicle maintenance and repairs. Maintain clean home and clean clothes for family. Plan and create dinners to entertain mate's employers, colleagues, clients, and prospects. Collaborate with mate to manage investments.

Clearly, creating a home and nurturing others require a variety of skills. It is obvious to any reader that many of these skills are transferable to paid work. Thus, there is no reason to omit or otherwise disguise or downplay the role of homemaker on your résumé. Rather than hide it, tell it—tell employers this important element of your unique story.

A Special Note to Veterans

Write for readers who have little or no understanding of the military. Use plain English civilian terminology.

As you write, omit/exclude:

- Military terminology/jargon
- Military acronyms
- Military slang
- Military abbreviations
- Details of combat

Since you are transitioning into a new career, include a Goal section (see page 21).

Create position descriptions/blurbs containing plenty of action statements (i.e., evidence of transferable skills)* and get specific. For example:

---

*Go to *www.google.com* or *www.alltheweb.com* and search for "military to civilian skills" until you find among the search results free translation sites providing military position descriptions and the civilian versions of those descriptions. Do not cut and paste the material from such sites into your résumé. Instead, use the information as food for thought as you devise civilian-friendly action statements for your unique document.

- Number of people managed
- Dollar amounts of budgets managed
- Dollar value of assets you managed
- "Civilian-transferable" skills training you have *given* to others
- Problems/opportunities successfully identified and acted upon
- Security clearances given to you (e.g., high-risk public trust, confidential, secret, or top secret)

In an Education section, include training you have *received*, but be selective. For example, omit training in marksmanship (unless you seek law enforcement work) and hand-to-hand combat, but include courses in logistics, technology, or the many other areas readily transferable to civilian work.

Find and carefully review any written evaluations you have received; these often contain useful food for thought when writing a résumé.

When getting your résumé reviewed (see item 8 on page xvii), be sure to get civilian reviewers. Ex-military people who have successfully transitioned to civilian career paths can make excellent reviewers, too, provided they meet the criteria in item 8 on page xvii.

Many free career resources for veterans are available on the Web. For example, go to *click4careercoaching.com*, click on "Use My Great Job Links and Job Hotlines," and see the "Links for Persons Transitioning from the U.S. Military."

If you have less than an honorable discharge (e.g., general, undesirable, bad conduct, or dishonorable), there is a chance you can have your discharge upgraded by the Discharge Review Board or Board of Correction of Military Records of the appropriate branch of service. Contact your local legal service agency (e.g., Legal Aid Society) or Red Cross, Veterans Center, or State Division of Veterans' Affairs for help. Doing so can improve your chances with employers who request your discharge papers.

Before applying for a discharge upgrade, be sure to request, obtain, and carefully save copies of your military records from Military Personnal Records Center, 9700 Page Avenue, St. Louis, MO 63132-1547. This is important because after you apply for a discharge upgrade, your records are sealed forever; neither you nor your attorney may view them.

Old discharge papers (form DD-214) include "SPN" or "spin" numbers that can identify people with drug or alcohol problems. Many employers can translate the spin numbers, so if these are issues for you, also request from St. Louis copies of the DD-214 with the spin number deleted.

A Special Note to Ex-Offenders

Ex-offenders searching for work face plenty of challenges. What is the biggest one?

- Being banned from receiving food stamps or other financial assistance? No.
- Being banned from taking some jobs (e.g., security, medicine, childcare, education)? No.
- Being unfairly discriminated against by many narrow-minded employers? No.
- Recovering from substance abuse?* No.
- Finding stable housing? No.
- Getting access to transportation? No.
- Getting access to health care? No.
- Improving basic skills?** No.
- Finding interview/work clothes?† No.

---

*See "A Special Note to People in Recovery" on pp. 113–114.

**Free courses are available. Go to any public library and ask for information about Adult Basic Education (ABE), General Educational Development (GED), or English for Speakers of Other Languages (ESOL).

†Free interview/work clothes are available. Go to any public library and ask for information about Bottomless Closet, Career Closet, Career Gear, Dress for Success, Working Wardrobes, and other like-minded organizations.

- Re-unification with loved ones? No.
- The belief that no employer will hire you because you are an ex-offender? Yes.

Believing that no employer will hire you because you are an ex-offender is your single biggest barrier to finding legal paid work. If you believe no employer will hire you because you are an ex-offender, you might as well stop reading; none of the following information will be of any use to you until you choose to change this belief.

Choosing to change negative beliefs is important. Drama inside your head can make it hard to believe in yourself. If you often have negative thoughts, argue, feel stressed, sad, or angry, there are ways to make it better. Ask your probation/parole officer to refer you to a clinical social worker or other mental health professional trained in rational emotive behavior therapy or cognitive behavioral therapy to help people think in ways that help them feel and do better. How you think about the job search (or anything else, for that matter) deeply affects results.

Once you believe—or act as if you believe until you really do believe—that an employer will hire you, it is time to create a résumé that will honestly get your phone to ring.

As mentioned in item number 1 on page xiv, don't make stuff up. There are many reasons to not make stuff up on your résumé or on a job application. If you lie and an employer finds out, you will very likely be immediately dismissed and maybe even criminally prosecuted for "willful misrepresentation." How can an employer find out? The information may slip out. Anyone who knows or recognizes you may (1) unintentionally communicate something that reveals your offense to your employer, (2) intentionally reveal, or (3) threaten to reveal. You do not need a secret and a potential crisis hanging over your head every day.

Therefore, do not write false starting dates or ending dates (see page 6) to mask the time during which you were incarcerated. Instead, write real starting and ending dates (month and year) and focus on including on your résumé all the transferable skills you have to offer. Prior to or while serving your sentence, did you get any vocational training? Did you work? Are you skilled in woodworking, carpentry, plumbing, painting, cleaning, electrical, metal work, food prep or cooking, landscaping, office equipment (phone, fax, copier, or computer), bookkeeping? Did you take any classes? Can you speak, read, or write a language other than English? Have you done volunteer work? In what ways did you participate in pre-release programs? Honestly list your accomplishments on your résumé and on job applications.

As you transition to the job market:

- Act as if you believe—until you really do believe—an employer will hire you.

- Create—alone or with help—an honest résumé. Do not be persuaded otherwise.

- Get a disposition slip for each offense from the court of conviction so you are ready for an employer's request.

- Rap sheets often contain damaging mistakes. Request a copy of yours from the appropriate state agency, review it, and then submit original disposition slips to correct the record.

- Ask people who can attest to how your behaviors have changed for the better to serve as references. See pages 75–76. If you're playing by the rules, then your parole officer can serve as an excellent reference.

- Think about, write, and rehearse in front of a mirror at least 100 times your three-part, sixty-second explanation of (1) your errors in judgment, (2) the lessons you've learned from these errors, and (3) your total commitment to a new path.

- Ask your local librarian for information on and forms for the Work Opportunity Tax Credit, and bring the forms to interviews. Give the forms to employers and explain that in addition to getting a good worker, if they hire you they can also get money (up to $2,400 at the time of this writing) from the government.

- Contact your state division of parole or, if you still have one, ask your parole officer to help you obtain certificates of rehabilitation (e.g., relief from disabilities, good conduct) that remove some restrictions on employment.

- Ask your local librarian (or call 1-877-872-5627) for information on and forms for the Federal Bonding Program. Bring this information and the forms to interviews, too. Use your judgment. If you think it will help, give the forms to employers and explain that this program helps protect employers (at no cost to them) against loss of money or property due to employer dishonesty.

- Avoid spending time with anyone who is engaged in illegal behaviors.

- Reach out to other ex-offenders who have successfully returned to legal paid work.

A Special Note to People in Recovery

As you know, you cannot move successfully along any career path if you are using. Before you attempt to create a résumé, seek out useful tools for recovery.

One such tool is relapse prevention training. Be your own advocate; ask around until you find it. Such training will help you understand the process that can lead to relapse, identify triggers, and learn coping skills to prevent relapse.

Another proven resource is *http://smartrecovery.org*, an excellent site that provides online mutual-help groups, an online message board, and information on face-to-face meetings around the world.

Here are three more excellent resources:

1. *When AA Doesn't Work for You: Rational Steps to Quitting Alcohol* by Albert Ellis and Emmett Velten (Fort Lee, N.J.: Barricade Books, 1992).

2. *Rational Recovery: The New Cure for Substance Addiction* by Jack Trimpey (New York: Pocket Books, 1996).

3. *Stay Sober and Straight: How to Prevent Addiction Relapse with the Rational Self-Help Treatment Method* by Maxie Maultsby (Weirton, W.Va.: Rational Self-Help Books, 1990).

Unexplained job exits, lengthy employment gaps, and other challenging issues caused by your substance abuse are more easily explained when you are *in* recovery. If the résumé you send includes clear evidence of skills useful to an employer, then you may be invited to explain the issues. Think about, write, and rehearse in front of a mirror at least 100 times your three-part, sixty-second explanation to:

- Acknowledge your total responsibility for the consequences of your substance abuse.
- Announce the period of time you have been clean—and your willingness to be tested.
- State your determination to continue to work at it for the rest of your life to stay clean.

Many employers respect the courage it takes to say and mean such things. As a result, people in recovery who are honestly committed to staying clean are hired and thriving in the workplace every day. You can be one of them.

Index

About the Author

Scott Bennett has read tens of thousands of résumés, conducted thousands of interviews, and hired and developed hundreds of employees at all levels in small, mid-size, and large organizations. In 1996, he transitioned from his role as President and Chief Operating Officer of Public Service Computer Software, Inc., into career coaching. Individually and in seminars and workshops, he has coached more than 4,000 job seekers from more than 100 countries. After launching the Career Services Office at Baruch College School of Public Affairs in New York City, he developed *click4careercoaching.com* to provide free information, tools, and resources for active career seekers.

Bennett earned a B.S. in Economics from Clark University, an M.S. in Education (specializing in Counseling and Personnel Services) from Fordham University, an M.S.W. from Hunter College School of Social Work, and an Advanced Post-Masters Certificate in Rational Emotive Behavior Therapy from Albert Ellis Institute. He lives in New York City.